# PENNY-WISE, PARTY-PERFECT DINNERS

## by The Good Cooking School

*Published by* J. G. Ferguson Publishing Company
*Chicago*
*Distributed to the Book Trade by*
*Doubleday & Company, Inc.*

# PREFACE

The Good Cooking School, founded in 1973, is the first association of its kind. Its members include owner-chefs of great three-star restaurants of France; executive chefs, restaurant owners and consultants to restaurant chains in the United States, England, and on the Continent; eminent cookbook authors, writers, editors and columnists, teachers, lecturers, and demonstrators specializing in information on food and wine. Its purpose is to expand the knowledge and appreciation of good eating, drinking and entertaining.

Under the banner of The Good Cooking School a variety of unusual and innovative programs have been initiated, including this book and a previous volume, *The Great Cooks Cookbook.* Another project, now in preparation for publication in the Fall of 1975, is the first catalogue ever assembled of the finest cooking tools of the world, an annotated selection of 1,500 implements from some 40,000 surveyed.

The purpose of this book is to prove that you don't have to spend a lot of money to eat well. By shopping carefully and using money-saving skills and techniques, you can create meals that are at once delicious and economical and that will delight your family as well as guests. The suggested menus, all reasonable in cost, are ideal for a wide range of dinner parties, from the very casual to the very formal. In planning the menus our 23 authors were careful to avoid the pitfalls hosts and hostesses often fall into: economizing on the main course while splurging on the dessert or appetizer. A total cost of ingredients is given for each dinner; but it must be stressed that the totals are relative, based on local costs as of December, 1974. Such things as geography, seasonality, supermarket specials, etc. can lower or raise costs. Along with many of the dinner recipes, a Bonus Recipe is given that uses the ingredients in or the leftovers from the primary menu as the basis for one or more courses of another meal. A reasonably priced wine that goes particularly well with each dinner is suggested where applicable.

Members of The Good Cooking School find today's conundrum—how to eat better for less—an exciting challenge. It is not really a question of *how much* the ingredients for a meal cost but, rather, with what subtlety and imagination they can be combined into dishes that are flavorful and appealing.

—Burton Richard Wolf

# CONTENTS

## ADELINE GARNER SHELL

# Guidelines for Careful Food Shoppers

You can save up to 30 percent on your bills right now—as high as food prices are—if you will put into practice these guidelines for more effective food shopping.

For some of us, it may mean extra time, effort and learning of facts and skills. But be assured—sensible buying is possible and it isn't difficult. Once you have the know-how, careful shopping becomes second nature. As food costs go down, eating pleasure goes up. In addition, the consumer awareness developed spills over to purchases other than food. Before you realize it, you develop an alertness that makes the marketplace work *for* you rather than against you.

Adeline Garner Shell *served as Director of the Bureau of Consumer Services for the New York City Department of Consumer Affairs, and currently is Guest Lecturer and Consultant on Consumerism at the University of Wisconsin-Stout and Adjunct Lecturer at Brooklyn College. A former magazine food editor, public health nutritionist and home agent, Ms. Shell is the author of* Supermarket Counter Power. *She lives in New York City.*

## LEARN GOOD NUTRITION TO GET MOST FROM YOUR DOLLAR

It is not the amount of food one buys for the money spent that is most important. What really counts is how much good nutrition you get for the money spent. Even at today's high prices you can eat better for less. Brush up your nutrition know-how. Plan family meals and shopping lists, using the following good eating chart:

### Daily Basic Nutrition Chart

*Milk Group*

Three or more 8-ounce glasses milk daily — Children
Four or more glasses daily — Teen-agers
Two or more glasses daily — Adults

Cheese, ice cream, and other milkmade foods should be counted in above amounts.

1 slice (1 ounce) American cheese equals ¾ glass milk.

½ cup creamed cottage cheese equals ⅓ glass milk.

½ cup (¼ pint) ice cream equals ¼ glass milk.

2 tablespoons cream cheese equal 1 tablespoon milk.

*Protein Group*

Two or more small to medium servings daily
Fish, poultry, eggs, cheese or meat as well as protein alternates such as dry beans, peas, nuts and peanut butter when served with or in combination with small amounts of the previously listed foods.

A small to medium serving is 2 to 3 ounces of cooked lean, boneless meat. About 1 pound solid, boneless meat makes six 2-ounce servings or four 3-ounce servings when cooked. Two eggs, 2 ounces of American or cheddar cheese, or ⅓ cup cottage cheese may be used instead of two ounces cooked meat. When using 1 cup cooked beans or 2 rounded tablespoons of peanut butter, combine with a small amount of the foods listed above, or serve when milk or milk pudding is part of meal.

■ *Note: Although milk is in previous group, it is also a good protein food.*

### Vegetable and Fruit Group

Four or more servings daily
Include a dark green leafy or deep yellow-orange vegetable and a citrus fruit, tomatoes or other good source of vitamin C daily.

A serving is ½ cup or more; or a medium apple, peach, banana, tomato or potato; or half a medium grapefruit or cantaloupe.

### Bread and Cereal Group

Four or more servings daily
Whole grain or enriched breads, cereals and cereal foods such as cornmeal, grits, macaroni, spaghetti, noodles, rice.

One serving is 1 slice bread; or ½ to ¾ cup of cooked cereal including macaroni, spaghetti, rice, etc.; or ¾ to 1 cup ready-to-eat cereal.

For those who want reliable nutrient information, send 85¢ to: Consumer Information, Public Documents Distribution Center, Pueblo, Colorado 81009 for the booklet, "Nutritive Value of Foods," 41 pp., 1971.

For further nutrition know-how, check references available in the local library and/or contact your local Cooperative Extension Service home agent for more detailed booklets on basic nutrition.

### LEARN TO COOK FROM SCRATCH

Today, what many people call "cooking" is really just mixing and matching one or more expensive convenience foods with a basic food—meat, for example. When this is done, people are paying others for cutting, slicing, grating, washing, seasoning, mixing, chopping, and full or partial cooking of foods for heating at home. When people do all these things themselves, they discover that their bill, depending on how many convenience foods were formerly used, is reduced by at least one-third. The extras when one cooks from scratch are real taste, better nutrition, and a decrease in the amount of questionable additives which many feel are not desirable or needed.

### BEWARE OF "BUDGET" RECIPES THAT ARE REALLY "BUDGET BUSTERS"

Watch those so-called "budget" recipes found in newspapers, magazines and food manufacturers' give-away leaflets. Most of the main dish recipes start out with a low-cost food. But you are directed to add such expensive items as canned mushrooms, canned soup, green or black olives, sour cream, meat and, for good measure, potatoes in the form of potato chips. Potato chips can cost you as much as $2.00 per pound depending on which size package you buy. Did you know that such recipes can often cost more than a good roast beef dinner before you finish?

For those of you who think that canned, creamed soup is cheap, just figure out what it costs to make a simple white sauce with dry, non-fat milk, flour and butter or margarine.

## DOUBLE CHECK THOSE COUPON OFFERS

Coupons are traffic builders, designed to lure you into the store to buy. Most coupon items are high priced, high profit products. They are heavily advertised brands, new products, and/or good sellers that are being undersold by another brand or store.

---

■ *Example: Coupon on brand name vegetable oil offered a savings of 15¢ on regular price of $2.35. In-store check showed another brand name vegetable oil selling for $2.05 without a coupon.*

---

When you take the time to check and compare, you'll learn (as well as earn) there are often non-coupon products that can be purchased for less money without loss in quality and eating pleasure. Big rule for coupon cutters: Make an in-store check before buying.

## EAT NOW—SHOP LATER

One survey shows that hungry shoppers spent $7.48 more than those who shopped after eating. So—be advised—have a good meal or snack before that next shopping trip to avoid impulse-buying on an empty stomach.

## MAKE IN-STORE CHECK OF SHOPPING LIST

There is no question that a shopping list saves money when it is based on the nutrition needs of family members, takes account of foods already on hand in the home, reflects a study of "specials" in more than one store ad, and represents a careful review of coupon offers. But don't be locked into your list. By following the "specials" and coupons, you may overlook some of the best basic food buys in the store.

---

■ *Example: The consumer who picked up the featured special of two (1-pound) cans of a name brand succotash for 86¢ missed the best buy. The alert consumer who did a routine in-store check came up with one can (1-pound) of the same brand of corn for 34¢ and one (1-pound) can of lima beans for 37¢, instead of the special, and was 15¢ richer. The lower priced succotash was easily prepared at home by just mixing the cans of corn and lima beans.*

---

Check and compare over a period of weeks and prove to yourself that the best food buys are rarely if ever featured in the food ads. You will soon learn that not all "specials" are best buys.

### READ THE LABELS TO UNDERSTAND THE NUTRITIVE VALUE OF FOODS

Get your food facts straight! Stop depending on advertising claims and public relations materials for the main source of information. Remember, words and photographs from these sources can be designed to confuse and blind consumers to actual nutrients and the amounts of nutrients found in foods. In addition, they never reveal any of the unfavorable or unwholesome aspects of a product.

Take the time to read labels to compare the actual nutritive value of foods. The alert consumer soon learns that when sugar is added to dry cereal, for example, the protein content of the cereal goes down. Look at the labels on your next visit to the store and you'll learn that 1 ounce of plain corn flakes has 2 grams protein while sugar-frosted corn flakes has 1 gram protein. But the alert shopper goes one step further. Check and compare other cereals in the store. For instance, a 1-ounce serving of oatmeal (approximately ⅓ cup uncooked or ⅔ cup cooked) has 4.2 grams protein. Compare the prices of the choices available and learn that oatmeal is the best nutrition buy. And it usually costs less than half, per serving, than the price of the sugared dry cereal!

## CUT OUT THE CUT-UPS AND SAVE

Almost always cut-up foods cost you more than buying the food whole. For example, when you buy boneless chicken breasts, you are giving the rest of the chicken to the butcher as a gift for the time and labor it took him to cut up the chicken!

Did you know, for example, that when you buy chicken steak, chuck filet steak, chuck club, and chuck stew, you are actually buying chuck blade steak cut up? When you buy a lean beef chuck blade steak weighing about 3 pounds and cut it up yourself into 1 chicken steak, 1 chuck filet steak, 1 chuck club steak, beef stew, and use the bones and meat scraps for broth, you save up to $1.05 compared to buying the cuts and canned broth separately. This means that if you use two chuck steaks a week over a period of a year, you'll save almost $110.00 on your meat bill.

Once you start being your own cut-up artist, you'll watch your food costs go down.

## BUY FOOD—NOT PACKAGING

Start saving money—big money—by buying food rather than packaging. Remember, you can't eat packaging!

---

■ *Example: On the same day in the same store, parsley flakes in a can container and parsley flakes in a bottle, packed by the same manufacturer and marked the same net weight, sold for:*
   *canned parsley flakes    29¢*
   *bottled parsley flakes    49¢*

---

Simple, easy "package-watching" awareness puts 20¢ in your pocket rather than an additional 20¢ going to the already strained garbage dump!

## CAN YOU AFFORD TO PAY FOR A MAID?

Most people do not realize that when they buy convenience foods, they are paying for the wages of a part-time maid and, in some instances, the wages of a cook. Ask yourself: Can you really afford this? For example, when you buy that pop-it-in-the-oven frozen spinach soufflé, do you realize you could make over double the amount yourself for almost half the amount it cost for that built-in service?

Take the time to figure the cost of frozen vegetables packaged with a little butter sauce, and compare the price to that of a basic plain frozen vegetable. Is that small amount of service and the cost of the butter worth the difference in price?

### STOP SUPPORTING THE "SHAPE" TRAP

One of the easiest ways for the manufacturer to increase prices is to change the shape or form of the basic food product.

Rolls are an example of the shape trap. When you compare the price of a 1-pound compact loaf bread that sells for 57¢ to a 1-pound package of rolls made by the same manufacturer from a similar recipe, you find that the rolls cost you $1.39. Again, stop and think this way. Is the bread product in the form of rolls worth an additional 82¢?

Sometimes shapes can be altered without an increase in price to the manufacturer and store, but most of the time the production of such items costs more. Interestingly enough, even when there isn't an increase in manufacturing costs, a price increase is felt by the consumer when the product is "new" or "special." That is another trap—newness and specialness.

### WATCH THE WEIGHT TO GAIN MONEY

Weights and measure reports made by qualified government inspectors show costly overcharges are paid by consumers when there is a difference between the actual weight and the weight marked on the package. One report showed 177 violations of short weight in a single meat market. It was estimated that the consumers who purchased these meats would have been overcharged from 5¢ to 40¢ per purchase.

When you buy prepackaged foods, such as meat or salad greens, which you suspect are less in weight than stated on the package, ask a clerk to reweigh the item before you pay for it. If you live in an area where a consumer scale is required by law, check for yourself.

If you find an error, check with a clerk and request a change in price.

### BEWARE THE SHORT-COUNT

A recent newspaper survey confirms that short-counting may be so widespread as to represent a considerable drain on the already strained consumer budget.

For example, when you get only 12 of the 14 ½-ounce cartons of mini-snack raisins, you lose over 8¢; when you get 5 packs of potato sticks in a package marked 6, you lose 10¢; and when you get 9 packets of instant oatmeal when the package is marked 10, you lose over 5¢.

Be your own counter of count-packaged food items.

### PAY SPECIAL ATTENTION AT THE REGISTER TO PRICES CHARGED FOR "SPECIALS"

Often clerks and checkers are not aware of the price for "specials" and ring up the regular amount. Consumer alertness at the register and a polite reminder to the clerk pay off rather than rip off.

### CHECK CASH REGISTER TAPES

When there is an overcharge at the cash register—regardless of the reason—it is money out of your pocket. Watch the register as the clerk rings up each item. Also, as soon as you get home, do a quick check of the items purchased against the register tape. In time, incorrect charges can add up to dollars. When there are overcharges, report them to the manager of the store. The store will make adjustments when a customer presents supporting evidence that an overcharge has been made.

It may be worth your effort to check the *total* of the tapes on your larger orders as well. Recently a team of inspectors posing as consumers went to a store and selected two different cartloads of groceries. They took their carts to separate checkout counters, purchased the food, and then examined the cash register tapes in the store. The price of each item in their carts was correctly posted on the tapes. However, when they took these tapes to an adding machine and computed the totals of their individual purchases, they found that they had each been overcharged by $3.55. The cash registers had been manipulated so that all customers with large orders would be overcharged $3.55!

### STOP FEEDING THE GARBAGE PAIL

To save money on food, learn how to clean, prepare and store food so you have the least waste. Become a real "how-to" food expert by brushing up on kitchen skills.

For example, when fresh broccoli is selling for 49 to 59¢ a bunch, you can get 2 to 2½ times the amount of broccoli by buying fresh rather than frozen, *if* you know how to prepare it for cooking with the least waste. Many cooks cut away the leaves and most of the stalk, and feed that to the garbage pail. The skilled cooks know that after soaking and washing the broccoli, you trim away only the dried-out portion of the stalk ends and only the bruised portion of the leaves.

Using drippings and fats from meat roasts, baked chicken, and soups as ingredients in white sauces and flavored rice dishes saves enough to pay for a home lunch. For example, making your own beef-flavored rice using fat and drippings from beef roast rather than using prepackaged beef-flavored rice cuts the cost from $1.20 a pound to 52¢—a savings of 68¢.

Another 63¢ is saved when you use bones from chuck steak (or other beef bones) to make beef broth rather than buying two cans of beef broth.

### RETURN THE SPOILS

Take the time to return food that is spoiled. If you cannot do this within a reasonable amount of time, call the manager of the store to explain the problem and ask for a credit.

With prepackaging there has been an increase in food spoilage. If you do not speak up, it costs you money!

## JAMES A. BEARD

# An Unfailingly Popular Beef Menu

**MENU**

Cup of Broth
Pot-au Feu
Irish Whole-Wheat Soda Bread
Lemon Snow with Custard Sauce

Total Cost of Dinner for 6: $10.40

Bonus Recipe: Cold Beef Salad

Wine: Côtes-du-Rhône
*(Cost not included)*

James A. Beard *is one of the country's most distinguished food experts. He is the author of 17 books, including* Beard on Bread, American Cookery, *and the now classic* How to Eat Better for Less Money, Hors d'Oeuvres and Canapés, *and* James Beard's Fish Cookery. *His most recent book,* Beard on Bread, *was published in 1974. A co-founder of The Good Cooking School, Inc., Mr. Beard conducts one of the most successful cooking schools in the United States. He appears frequently on television and acts as a consultant to numerous food and drink companies throughout the world.*

his menu is planned to be a Sunday lunch with, hopefully, a few leftovers; or it could be Saturday night dinner that might include one or two guests. It's inexpensive, it's very nutritious and, I find, unfailingly popular.

I use a most inexpensive cut of meat for the pot-au-feu. It's the shin, or *gite,* which is often used in France. This cut is from the foreleg of the steer and is meaty and gelatinous. It cooks to a nice tenderness with, what delights me, the lovely gelatinous quality emphasized and it produces a most pleasant broth because of that. It's not the most perfect meat for slicing but you *can* get nice even slices if you do not overcook it. That which is left will make a perfectly delicious beef salad or a good hash.

We're serving the vegetables that are used to flavor the pot-au-feu. We're not cooking the vegetables the entire time we cook the pot-au-feu except for those we need to add flavor to our broth. Naturally the broth in the first course is from the pot-au-feu. The traditional accompaniments for this dish are coarse salt, tiny cornichons—the very sour pickles of France—and mustard.

The Irish soda bread speaks for itself.

The dessert is light, easy and inexpensive—a lemon snow.

## POT-AU-FEU

Wipe the shin with a damp cloth to remove any bits of bone left from the sawing. Place it in a deep 8 to 9-quart pot with 1 carrot, 1 large onion (stuck with 2 cloves if you wish), 1 bay leaf, 1½ teaspoons thyme, ½ teaspoon summer savory. If you bought a piece of fennel, you should add the trimmings from the head, or if you bought celery, add the celery leaves to the pot and let them be used for flavor.

Dislodge the marrow from the marrow bones, place in a piece of waxed paper or foil and set aside. Put the bones in with the meat and the seasonings. Cover with water, about an inch above the meat. Bring to a boil. Skim off any scum that rises to the surface for the first five minutes. Add 2 to 3 teaspoons of salt and about 1½ teaspoons of freshly ground black pepper. Let it boil vigorously for 10 minutes. Reduce the heat

*6–7 pounds shin of beef, with a goodly amount of meat on it*
*1 carrot*
*1 large onion*
*1 bay leaf*
*1½ teaspoons thyme*
*½ teaspoon summer savory*
*1 head of fennel (optional)* †
*2–3 marrow bones*
*2–3 teaspoons salt*
*1½ teaspoons freshly ground black pepper*
*6 medium onions, peeled*
*6 carrots, scraped*

*† If fennel is not in the market, you may use a stalk*

Chopped chives or parsley
Cornichon (*optional*)
Horseradish (*optional*)

*of celery or you may use a
few turnips instead of the
fennel. However, the fennel
gives a novel and delicious
flavor.*

and simmer for about 1½ to 2 hours. At the end of 1½ hours, test the meat for tenderness and taste the broth for seasoning. It may well need more salt and it might need a touch more pepper. If by chance you do not have the fennel or the celery and did buy turnips, you could add those at this time, peeled and quartered.

Return the cover to the pot and continue simmering until meat is tender. Gauging about 30 to 45 minutes before the time for your meat to be taken out, add the 6 onions and the 6 carrots and the head of fennel, cut into quarters, or the celery cut into quarters, to your pot and let them cook until they are just tender. *Do not overcook them.* When the meat is tender, you may remove it even though the vegetables may take a few more minutes of cooking. Place meat on a warm platter and put it in a warm place. Cover with a bowl or with foil to keep warm.

### The Broth

Now, extract about 6 cups of the broth from the pot and place it in a saucepan and skim any fat that may rise to the surface. Taste it very thoroughly for seasoning. Bring it to a boil again, and again skim off any fat that may be on the surface. Cut the pieces of marrow that you have set aside into thin slices and reserve. Set up either 6 bouillon cups or 6 good-sized coffee cups for your first course.

While the pot-au-feu is cooking, you will naturally have made your Irish soda bread so that it comes out at least ¾ of an hour before your pot-au-feu or your broth. When your broth is ready to serve, toss the marrow slices into it for just 2 or 3 minutes, then ladle it into the cups and add to it a goodly sprinkling of chopped chives, if they are in season, or chopped parsley. Serve with melba toast or the soda bread.

### The Pot-au-feu

When you and your guests have finished the broth, it's time to serve the pot-au-feu. Arrange the meat on a platter. I rather like to slice it before I serve it and surround it with the carrots and onions and either the celery or the fennel and give it a sprig or two of parsley; garnish the platter with some of the sour cornichons from France around the edge and some freshly grated horseradish, if you have it. Serve the meat with the vegetables and the Irish soda bread and pass a selection of mustards.

It's a hearty, good dish and it is improved if you bring in a small bowl of the broth and spoon a spoon or two of broth over each plate as it is served. It gives it added distinction.

### IRISH WHOLE-WHEAT SODA BREAD *

Irish whole-wheat soda bread, thinly sliced, has a great, heart-warming quality about it that goes perfectly with this type of meal.

*3 cups whole-wheat flour (it should be coarse)*
*1 cup all-purpose flour*
*1 tablespoon salt (if you use coarse salt, or 2 teaspoons if you use ordinary kitchen salt)*
*1 level teaspoon baking soda*
*¾ teaspoon double-acting baking powder*
*1½–2 cups buttermilk*
*Sweet butter*

Combine the dry ingredients and mix thoroughly to distribute the soda and baking powder, then add enough buttermilk to make a soft dough, similar in quality to biscuit dough but firm enough to hold its shape. Knead for a few minutes on a lightly floured board until quite smooth and velvety. Form into a round loaf and place in a well-buttered 8-inch cake pan or a well-buttered cookie sheet. Cut a cross on the top of the loaf with a very sharp, floured knife.

Bake in a preheated 375 F. oven for about 35 to 40 minutes, or until the loaf is nicely browned and sounds hollow when rapped with the knuckles. (The cross will have spread open, which is characteristic of soda bread.) Let the loaf cool before slicing very thin; soda bread must never be cut thick.

Serve with plenty of sweet butter.

### LEMON SNOW WITH CUSTARD SAUCE

In saucepan, sprinkle gelatin over ½ cup of cold water. Place over medium heat; stir constantly until gelatin dissolves (2 or 3 minutes). Remove from heat. Add sugar and salt; stir until dissolved. Add remaining ¾ cup cold water, lemon rind and juice. Chill, stirring occasionally, until mixture is slightly thicker than consistency of unbeaten egg white. Turn into large bowl of electric mixer; add egg whites. Beat at high speed until mixture begins to hold its shape, 7 to 10 minutes. Turn into 6-cup serving bowl or mold, or into individual

*1 envelope unflavored gelatin*
*1¼ cups cold water*
*¾ cup sugar*
*⅛ teaspoon salt*
*1 teaspoon grated lemon rind*
*¼ cup lemon juice*
*2 unbeaten egg whites*

* From BEARD ON BREAD by James A. Beard. Copyright © 1973 by James A. Beard. Reprinted by permission of Alfred A. Knopf, Inc.

serving dishes. Chill until firm. Serve with Custard
Sauce (recipe below).

## CUSTARD SAUCE

1½ cups milk
2 egg yolks
1 whole egg
3 tablespoons sugar
⅛ teaspoon salt
1 teaspoon vanilla

Scald milk in top of double boiler. In small bowl, beat
egg yolks and whole egg with sugar and salt only until
blended. Gradually add small amount of hot milk, stirring constantly. Add egg mixture to double boiler and
cook, stirring constantly, over hot (not boiling) water
until mixture coats a metal spoon. Remove from heat;
pour into bowl and cool. Stir in vanilla.

### ■ *Bonus Recipe*
### COLD BEEF SALAD

4 cups cold boiled beef, cut
into ¾–1-inch dice
2 cups green onions, thinly
sliced
2 cups celery, thinly sliced
1 cup green pepper,
shredded
2 cups boiled potatoes,
thinly sliced
2 cups tomatoes, peeled and
cut into wedges, or 2 cups
cherry tomatoes
¼ cup parsley, chopped
¼ cup capers
1 cup raw mushrooms,
thinly sliced
1 cup or more mustard
flavored Vinaigrette Sauce
Romaine or chicory leaves
6 hard-boiled eggs, halved
Parsley sprigs
Olives

In a mixing bowl combine the first nine ingredients and
toss lightly with the Vinaigrette Sauce.* Arrange romaine and chicory leaves around a serving ravier or a
bowl, and heap the tossed mixture into the center. Top
with the hard-boiled eggs, a few parsley sprigs, and
olives. Serves 4 to 6.

* See page 94 for Mustard Vinaigrette recipe.

## ELIZABETH BEVIN BENSON

# French Cooking Is Economical

**MENU**

Cauliflower Cream Soup
Sautéed Chicken with Carrots
Cold Chocolate Soufflé

Total Cost of Dinner for 6: $11.54

Bonus Recipe: Chicken Wing Drumsticks Provençal

Wine: French Bordeaux *or* California Cabernet Sauvignon
*(Cost not included)*

Elizabeth Bevin Benson *teaches the fundamentals of French cuisine at her own school, The Essex Whaler, in Essex, Connecticut. Born in New York City, she has lived in France, Spain, Switzerland and Argentina, all of whose varied cuisines she has mastered. These will soon be represented in her cookbook in process. She recently completed the translation of the monumental* Ali-Bab Encyclopedia of Practical Gastronomy, *published in 1974.*

he French are a thrifty people. Economy is natural to them and waste is abhorrent—waste of food most particularly. Every scrap of food has a use—for people, for livestock and, finally, as compost. Unfortunately, much stress has been put on "haute cuisine" which is very costly in that it requires expensive ingredients such as truffles or crayfish. Haute cuisine, however, is only a small part of traditional French cooking. It is in the basic French cuisine that we find the techniques and preparations that are economical and delicious.

Economy lies in the use of less expensive main ingredients, but there is no economy in poor quality food. It is wise to choose less costly cuts of meat, make extensive use of chicken, fish or eggs and take advantage of every sale, provided that the ingredients are fresh. The French have evolved an infinite number of variations on a basic theme which makes it possible to use these same main ingredients over and over again without tiring of the repetition. Investing in a few quality staples, such as unsalted butter, heavy cream, and some moderately priced cooking wines can help to create really luxurious fare from common and inexpensive main ingredients.

The Cauliflower Cream Soup, sautéed Chicken and dessert soufflé recipes that follow are all good examples of what one can create from a simple process that can be varied to taste.

## CAULIFLOWER CREAM SOUP

Wash, trim and separate head of cauliflower. Blanch flowerets in a large saucepan of boiling, salted water for 4 or 5 minutes. Drain and refresh under cold, running water. Set aside.

In the same saucepan melt the butter and blend in the flour. Cook and stir a minute or two until the flour has taken on a light golden color. Slowly whisk in the chicken broth and cook, uncovered, stirring until the mixture has thickened slightly. Add about 2 cups of the flowerets and cook them in the soup until tender.

Force the soup through a fine mesh sieve or a food mill. (If using a blender to purée the soup, use less of the cauliflowerets or a little more chicken broth so the soup will not be too thick.) Heat the soup again.

**Basic chicken velouté**

*6 tablespoons unsalted butter*
*6 tablespoons flour*
*6 cups chicken broth*
*(recipe page 20)*
*Salt and white pepper to taste*

**Vegetable and soup enrichments**

*1 small head of cauliflower*
*2 large egg yolks*
*½ cup heavy cream*

Beat the egg yolks, the cream and a little of the hot soup together in a small bowl. Add this mixture to the soup. Taste and correct the seasoning with salt and white pepper. Serve in a hot soup tureen garnished with thin slivers of partly cooked cauliflower.

■ *Variations: A whole range of soups can be made using the same basic chicken velouté that we use here. Vegetables such as carrots, Brussels sprouts, cabbage, string beans, or spinach can be used in place of the cauliflower.*

*To make a hearty soup to serve as a main dish with salad and dessert, add quite a few whole cauliflowerets a few minutes before serving; heat and serve.*

### SOME THOUGHTS ON CHICKEN

The chicken is one of the few birds that they claim cannot fly, but it certainly makes its way around the kitchen. It has so many assets: low cholesterol, high protein, lovely texture, pleasant taste. It was once idolized by certain civilizations—an honor which, some wit noted, did not prevent it from being eaten!

When there are sales on chicken, it is advisable to buy as many as six at one time and set aside a couple of hours to cut them up and freeze the parts individually —thighs, drumsticks, breasts, filet mignons, wing drumsticks, livers, gizzards and fat. Freeze these in separate plastic bags and use the carcasses and wing tips to make strong chicken stock. This can be boiled down and frozen in separate containers for future use.

From basic chicken broth or sautéed chicken (recipes follow), for example, delicious, economical variations are endless. It is the taste dimension to a basic recipe that is the touchstone of French cuisine.

### CHICKEN BROTH

In a 3-quart saucepan put the carcasses, wing flaps and skin from a raw chicken and cover with cold water. Bring rapidly to a boil and skim off the rising scum for the next 5 minutes. Then add 1 carrot, 1 onion, 1 bay leaf, a few parsley stems, a pinch of dried thyme (or some fresh if available), 6 peppercorns and salt to taste. Simmer as long as possible to extract as much flavor as possible. You will need 6 cups of broth for the basic chicken velouté (preceding recipe) so add water, or boil down, accordingly. If the broth does not seem strong enough, add 1 or 2 packets of MBT chicken broth powder (do not use bouillon cubes). Skim off as much of the surface fat as possible before using.

## BASIC CHICKEN SAUTÉ

Sautéed chicken has provided the basis for many of the very famous French dishes. *Larousse Gastronomique* lists 138 of them and there are hundreds more. It stands to reason, then, that by mastering the very simple procedures involved in preparing basic sautéed chicken, any cook can prepare a whole gamut of dishes by varying the wines, seasonings or garnishes. The chicken pieces can be sautéed ahead of time, sauced, and then held until ready to be reheated or finished at meal time. Some of the chicken sautées are actually better held overnight.

Cut up the chicken or chickens into individual serving pieces: two thighs, two drumsticks, four breast pieces (two breast halves cut in two), two wing drumsticks and two wing tips, plus carcass and back.

The carcass and wings may be sautéed and used as a bed for arranging the other pieces or they may be reserved for broth and the wing drumsticks for individual sautéeing.

The chicken can either be skinned or not. If it is to be served fairly dry, with only a sprinkling of wine and pan juices, then the skin remains crisp and pleasant. If, however, the chicken is to be sauced, then the skin is best removed. To do this, grasp it firmly with a piece of paper towel and pull. It should peel off easily.

Rub the chicken pieces all over with a piece of cut lemon and dry thoroughly with paper toweling or they will not brown.

For fat, use: 2 tablespoons unsalted butter and 1 tablespoon corn oil

*or*      3 tablespoons olive oil

*or*      2 thickly sliced strips of bacon, cut up

The fat you use will depend on the final dish you are preparing. For the plain, basic chicken, use butter and corn oil. Place a large skillet over low to moderate heat, put in the dark meat pieces and sauté 4 or 5 minutes on one side, turn and brown on the other side 4 or 5 minutes. Then add the white meat (after removing the other pieces) and sauté 2 or 3 minutes per side only. You may have to raise the fire a little and possibly add a little more oil. When all the pieces are browned, return them to the pan, season to taste with salt and pepper, partially cover the pan and cook over low to moderate heat for another 15 or 20 minutes depending on the size of the chicken. Or, you can place the pan, uncovered, in a 350 F. preheated oven and bake it for 25 or 30 minutes. Turn chicken once or twice during the cooking time. Watch that it does not burn.

Arrange the chicken pieces on a hot platter. Pour ¼ cup white Vermouth into skillet, scrape and whisk to deglaze the skillet thoroughly. Add 1 tablespoon unsalted butter and when it is melted pour pan juices over chicken. Sprinkle with chopped parsley and serve.

For variation, flame chicken with cognac, add sherry or Madeira to pan along with freshly minced herbs (chives, tarragon, chervil or garlic, or a mixture) and finish as above.

### SAUTÉED CHICKEN WITH CARROTS

**Chicken**

*2 3–3½-pound chickens*
*2 tablespoons unsalted butter*
*1 tablespoon corn oil or peanut oil*
*Salt and pepper to taste*
*¼ cup brandy for flaming*
*1 cup Madeira wine*
*2 mashed garlic cloves*
*1 tablespoon tomato paste*
*1 tablespoon meat glaze (Bovril)*
*1 cup beef broth*
*1 tablespoon currant jelly*
*½ cup orange juice*
*1 tablespoon potato starch*

Cut up and sauté chickens in butter and oil as in the basic recipe (preceding) just for the preliminary browning time. Season with salt and pepper. (Save carcass and wing tips for broth [recipe page 20]; wing drumsticks for another meal (see Bonus Recipe page 24); liver and gizzard for pâté and ragôut.) When all the chicken pieces are browned, arrange them in the bottom of a large casserole and flame with the brandy.

Deglaze the sauté pan with the Madeira and stir in the garlic, tomato paste, meat glaze, beef broth, currant jelly and orange juice. Mix the potato starch with a small amount of water in a cup and whisk into the liquids, stirring and letting everything come to a boil over moderate heat. Boil for one minute until the potato starch has cooked and thickened slightly. The sauce will be fairly thin at this point.

Pour sauce over the chicken, making sure to coat all pieces well. Cover with a sheet of aluminum foil, then with the casserole cover so as to seal it as hermetically as possible. Place in a 350 F. preheated oven and cook 45 minutes. Or, alternately, place over low to medium heat, keeping the contents of the pan at a very slow simmer. Check occasionally and ladle sauce over chicken if necessary.

Scrape or peel the carrots. Slice them fairly thin. Cover with cold water and bring to a boil. Drain and return carrots to the pan along with 2 tablespoons butter and ½ cup of chicken broth or water. Season to taste with salt, pepper and lemon juice. Cover pan and cook gently until carrots are just tender. Keep them hot.

When chicken is ready to serve, spoon carrots on a hot platter, sprinkle generously with chopped parsley and arrange chicken pieces on top. Taste the pan juices to correct seasoning, if necessary, and check for thickness. If the sauce seems too thin, add another tablespoon of potato starch mixed with water and quickly boil the sauce until the potato starch has cooked and sauce has thickened. If the sauce is too thick, thin with a little Madeira, beef broth or orange juice. Pour hot sauce over chicken and carrots. Garnish platter with orange sections and more parsley.

**Carrots**

*6 large carrots*
*2 tablespoons unsalted butter*
*½ cup chicken broth (see recipe p. 20)*
*Salt and pepper to taste*
*Juice from ½ lemon*

**Garnish**

*Chopped parsley*
*1 small can mandarin orange sections or*
*1 large orange, peeled and sectioned*

■ *Variations: Use braised spinach or lettuce, or sliced, boiled sweet potatoes instead of carrots. Any of the squashes would be acceptable, either boiled and sliced or mashed. Light claret or sherry could substitute for the Madeira, and chicken broth used instead of beef broth. Each new combination would provide a whole new taste. Pineapple juice and pineapple chunks instead of the oranges would give you another new approach. In that one recipe exists a whole culinary repertoire.*

## COLD CHOCOLATE SOUFFLÉ

This is a very luxurious dessert and although perhaps not as economical as others that do not require heavy cream, it is nevertheless well within suitable range for an elegant but economical dinner party. It is economical in preparation time, and it can be prepared one or two days ahead of time, which is also a plus factor.

In the large bowl of an electric mixer, beat the eggs and yolks until frothy. Gradually add the sugar and salt and beat at fairly high speed for 12 minutes, until the mixture is light and thick.

Soften the gelatin in the Crème de Cacao in a very small pan. Place the pan in another with warm water and heat gently until the gelatin has dissolved. Do not

*3 whole eggs*
*2 large egg yolks*
*⅓ cup sugar*
*Pinch of salt*
*1½ tablespoons unflavored gelatin*
*⅓ cup Crème de Cacao*
*6 ounces dark, sweet chocolate, cut up into small pieces*
*2 tablespoons water*
*¾ cup heavy cream*
*1 teaspoon vanilla extract*
*⅓ cup heavy cream, whipped*

overheat. Cool slightly and gradually beat into the egg mixture.

In a small, heavy pan, melt the chocolate with 2 tablespoons water. Do this by placing the pan with the chocolate into a larger pan half filled with water. Bring the water gradually to a boil and remove from heat. Stir a few seconds until chocolate starts to melt, then let it rest and when it is melted stir vigorously. Melted chocolate should be smooth and velvetly, with no lumps or granulations. Beat the melted chocolate into the egg-gelatin mixture.

Whip the heavy cream until it holds peaks and fold into the above mixture along with the vanilla. Spoon into a medium-sized soufflé dish and chill.

Just before serving, whip the ⅓ cup of cream and pipe a decorative layer on top of the soufflé.

If desired use a smaller soufflé dish. Using corn oil, oil a double thickness of aluminum foil, wrap it around the outside of the soufflé dish so that it comes 3½ inches above the rim of the dish and tape it securely in place. Spoon the soufflé mixture into the dish and let it come two-thirds of the way up the aluminum foil. It will set firmly and before serving, you can carefully remove the foil. Decorate with whipped cream, as above.

■ *Variations: The basic mixture is simply eggs and sugar to which the main flavoring is added, along with gelatin for holding quality and heavy cream for richness. By varying the flavorings, one can come up with any number of luscious concoctions.*

*Here we use chocolate and Crème de Cacao. Consider using strawberry or raspberry pulp and Framboise as the liqueur; Grand Marnier and grated orange rind (or even Grand Marnier alone); instant coffee and a coffee liqueur; apricot pulp and apricot brandy; ground nutmeg and pumpkin pulp with rum or any suitable liqueur; or make up your own combinations!*

■ *Bonus Recipe*

**CHICKEN WING DRUMSTICKS PROVENÇAL**
Freeze chicken wing drumsticks each time you have a chicken until you have enough for one meal. When

ready to serve them, thaw, dry and sauté them in butter and oil until golden brown, seasoning with salt and pepper to taste (see recipe p. 21). They should take about 20 minutes. Remove to a hot platter, add 2 or 3 cloves of crushed garlic to pan, and sauté a minute or two, then deglaze pan with white Vermouth. Pour this over the chicken and serve generously sprinkled with chopped parsley.

## GRACE ZIA CHU

# A Complete Chinese Meal With Pork

**MENU**

Pork Slices with Chinese Cabbage Soup
Bean Sprouts with Pork and Egg Shreds
Red-Cooked Pork Cubes with Eggs
Boiled Rice

Total Cost of Dinner for 6: $7.50

Bonus Recipes: Steamed Sea Bass, Cucumber Salad

Wine: California Rosé
*(Cost not included)*

Grace Zia Chu, *author of* The Pleasures of Chinese Cooking, *is the foremost authority in the United States on the cuisines of China. She has taught Chinese cooking at the China Institute of America in New York City. Mme. Chu is a member of the faculty of The Good Cooking School.*

hinese cooking is exceptionally healthful, economical, time-saving and delicious, and this complete meal, a departure from the classic Chinese menu, is specially designed for economy and easy preparation.

A more conventional menu would include a variety of foods, of ways of cooking, and of ways of cutting. The selection might include meats in chunks prepared in the "red-stewed" way; a diced seafood dish cooked in its natural juices; vegetables prepared by stir frying; and a cold dish of some sort.

As you will note, pork is used throughout the menu —something never done at a Chinese table!—but it is not only tasty and nourishing, it is also economical. The cost of the entire meal comes to about $1.25 for each serving.

Unlike some Chinese dishes there is no last minute cooking. If partly cooked the day before, some of the congealed fat on top of the soup and the pork dish can be skimmed off, making them more wholesome dishes.

It is best to buy a whole piece of pork butt, about 5½ pounds, and have the butcher cut the bone into two pieces. The rest is easy to handle. Just follow the recipes and cut the meat to the amount desired.

For those who prefer to vary the menu courses, we are including recipes for Steamed Sea Bass and Cucumber Salad, which call for a few additional ingredients but are still within our budget.

## PORK SLICES WITH CHINESE CABBAGE SOUP

Boil 2 quarts of water in a 4-quart saucepan. Add pork bone, ginger and scallion. Bring to boil again. Turn heat to low and simmer for an hour. Discard pork bone.

Slice ½ pound pork into slices 1 x 1 x ⅛-inch. Marinate in soy sauce and sherry for 15 minutes.

Wash and cut cabbage into inch pieces. Add to soup and bring to boil. Add salt and mix a few times. Add marinated pork slices and mix with fork or chopsticks to avoid meat slices sticking together. Cover; cook over medium heat for 10 minutes.

Sprinkle pepper over soup. Keep warm till ready to serve.

■ *Note: It is better to make the soup broth with the bone the day before. After cooling leave in refrigerator.*

*Pork bone from a 5-pound pork butt*
*2 slices fresh ginger, about the size of a 50¢ piece*
*1 stalk scallion, cut into 2-inch lengths*
*½ pound boneless pork butt (1 cup)*
*1 teaspoon dark soy sauce*
*1 teaspoon pale dry sherry*
*1½ pounds Chinese cabbage*
*2 teaspoons salt*
*⅛ teaspoon white pepper*

*On the day of using, skim off the fat on top. Then pro-
ceed to add cabbage and pork.*

### BEAN SPROUTS WITH PORK AND EGG SHREDS

*10 ounces boneless fresh
pork butt in 1 piece
1½ pounds fresh bean
sprouts
1 teaspoon vegetable oil
1 medium-sized egg slightly
beaten to mix the white and
yolk
1 stalk scallion*

**Sauce**

*3 tablespoons light soy
sauce
3 tablespoons wine vinegar
2 tablespoons oriental
sesame seed oil
1 teaspoon sugar*

Boil the piece of pork in 2 cups of cold water for 30
minutes.

Thoroughly cool the pork. Cut into slices about
1 x ¼-inch, then shred the slices into matchstick sizes
(makes about 1¼ cups).

Bring 4 cups of water to boil in a 2-quart saucepan.
Plunge bean sprouts into the boiling water. Turn heat
off. Let bean sprouts remain in the water for 3 minutes.
Rinse in cold water until chilled. Drain and set aside.

Heat oil in a frying pan. Pour in egg and swirl until
egg covers the entire surface of the pan. When egg sets,
slide it out onto a plate. Cool. Cut into julienne strips.
Set aside.

Cut the green part of the scallion into ¼-inch pieces.

Mix soy sauce, vinegar, sesame seed oil and sugar in
a bowl. Set aside for later use.

When ready to serve, mix the pork with the bean
sprouts. Pour the sauce into the mixture and mix thoroughly. Dish onto a serving plate. Top with egg strips
and then sprinkle scallion over all. Serve cold.

■ *Note: The piece of pork can be cooked with bone for
making soup (recipe page 29). Time for 30 minutes
and pick out from the soup broth. In this way the soup
gets the flavor of the pork. This could also be cooked a
day ahead.*

### RED-COOKED PORK CUBES WITH EGGS

*3 pounds boneless pork butt
6 medium-sized eggs
2 tablespoons vegetable oil
¾ cup pale dry sherry
6 tablespoons dark soy
sauce
4 teaspoons sugar
2 slices fresh ginger
2 stalks scallions, cut into
2-inch lengths*

Cut pork into 1-inch cubes (about 6 cups).

Hard boil the eggs. Cool and shell. Pierce through
horizontally with a peeling knife.

Heat 1 tablespoon oil in a wok or skillet. Add about
half of the pork. Turn quickly to seal the pork. Transfer to a 3-quart saucepan. Heat other tablespoon oil,
add other half pork and repeat process. Add to the
pork already in the saucepan. Turn heat on high and
begin to cook the pork. Add sherry, soy sauce, sugar,
ginger and scallions. Mix well. Add 1⅓ cups cold
water. Bring to boil. Cover; turn flame to medium and
cook for 20 minutes, mixing a few times. Then add

eggs, making sure that all eggs are submerged in the liquid.

Continue cooking for 25 minutes more. Serve warm with boiled rice (recipe follows).

■ *Note: It is even better to cook this dish a day ahead. Leave in the refrigerator overnight. Before rewarming on top of the range, be sure to skim off the fat on top of the pork. It can be frozen after it is completely cooked. When ready to use be sure to thaw to room temperature and warm on top of the range.*

## BOILED RICE

Place rice in a 2-quart saucepan that has a tight lid. Add water. Turn heat to high and bring to hard boil (about 3 to 4 minutes). Cover; turn heat to low and simmer for 20 minutes. Remove from heat. Without uncovering pan, let rice relax for another 20 minutes. Stir briskly with chopsticks or fork to loosen rice before serving.

*1 cup long grain rice*
*1⅓ cups cold water*

Makes 3 cups of cooked rice.

■ *Note: Leftover rice can be reheated in a double boiler the next day.*

■ *Bonus Recipes*

## STEAMED SEA BASS *

Clean and wash the sea bass. Dry inside and outside. Put whole fish into a heatproof dish.

Mix shredded fresh ginger root, scallion, black beans, soy sauce, dry sherry and oil. Pour mixture over fish.

In an 8-quart saucepan heat 2 quarts water until boiling. Place a rack in the saucepan and put the dish containing the bass on it. Be sure the water is even with the rack and no higher so that the water, when it boils again, will not get into the dish. Cover tightly and steam the fish for 15 minutes over a high flame. Serve immediately. (Serves 4)

*1 sea bass, about 1½ pounds*
*½ teaspoon fresh ginger root, shredded*
*1 scallion cut into 2-inch pieces*
*½ teaspoon fermented black beans ***
*1 tablespoon soy sauce*
*1 tablespoon dry sherry*
*1 tablespoon peanut or corn oil*

*\* Fermented black beans can be purchased at Chinese food stores. If you cannot locate them, substitute ½ teaspoon salt.*

■ *Note: Fish must be absolutely fresh for steaming. Fine-textured fish such as porgy, trout, butterfish, floun-*

* From The Pleasures of Chinese Cooking *by Grace Zia Chu (Simon and Schuster, Inc., New York, 1962).*

der, sole and white fish can all be steamed in the same manner as sea bass. Filets of any of the above fish can be steamed the same way and are easier to handle because they are smaller.

To serve Chinese style the fish must be brought to the table whole, including the head. If you prefer, however, remove the head before steaming the fish.

### CUCUMBER SALAD *

1 medium-sized cucumber
½ teaspoon salt
1 tablespoon wine vinegar
1 tablespoon soy sauce
1 tablespoon sugar
1 teaspoon oriental sesame seed oil *

* If sesame seed oil is not available, use a teaspoon of any salad oil. But sesame seed oil is the ingredient that makes the salad distinctive.

Peel the cucumber. Cut into very thin slices. Sprinkle with ½ teaspoon salt and let stand for 20 minutes. Drain.

In a bowl mix vinegar, soy sauce, sugar and sesame seed oil.

Pour sauce over the drained cucumber. Mix and serve cold. Serves 4.

■ *Note: Be sure sauce is mixed with the cucumber at the last minute in order to keep the color of the cucumber light.*

*Lettuce leaves, spinach leaves or shredded celery cabbage can be used in place of cucumber.*

*From* The Pleasures of Chinese Cooking *by Grace Zia Chu (Simon and Schuster, Inc., New York, 1962).*

## RUTH ELLEN CHURCH

# The Versatile Turkey

**MENU**

Tomato Slush
Roast Turkey with Cornbread Stuffing
Giblet and Mushroom Gravy
Mashed Rutabagas
Green Beans
Pink Grapefruit and Avocado Salad with Radish Chips
Poached Pears

Total Cost of Dinner for 6: $17.69

Bonus Recipes: Plantation Shortcake,
Turkey Curry on Rice, Turkey and Noodles Casserole

Wines: California Chablis, Gamay Beaujolais
*or* California Burgundy
(*Cost not included*)

Ruth Ellen Church, *a syndicated wine columnist for* The Chicago Tribune, *was Food Editor of the* Tribune *for more than thirty years when she retired in 1974. Author of seven cookbooks, her second wine book* Entertaining with Wines *will be published in 1975.*

love to roast a turkey, especially a very big one, because it makes so many bonus meals. Turkey sandwiches and casseroles, turkey curry, turkey salad or hash (the hash is great for a Sunday brunch) and, finally, turkey bone soup, a catch-all for salad greenery and vegetables left in the refrigerator, a hearty and delicious potful of good food which too often is wasted. Just for that feeling of virtuous thriftiness, the soup is worth the effort. And it really isn't that much effort!

Turkey is always a bargain when you consider its versatility. In the last few years the turkey grower hasn't made much money; indeed, he has taken some staggering losses because he has had to sell the big birds for less than the cost of their food.

Turkey is one of your best buys in meat at any time of the year. A survey has shown that 25 percent of consumers buy turkey the year round, but there are still too many who regard turkey as Thanksgiving fare only. This is shortsighted.

More than half of today's turkeys wind up as turkey parts, especially turkey rolls, or in products packaged, canned or frozen by food companies. In some markets turkey by the piece is available to the consumer; rarely, it can be found diced, ready for use in casseroles and salads.

I think that turkey can lose much of its flavor in the transition. The fullest turkey flavor comes from cooking the bird with skin and bones, as in roasting. Many turkeys are packaged with directions for roasting included; some have little thermometers embedded in their breasts which pop up when the turkey has cooked perfectly. Many turkeys now come with a "basting mix" injected which obviates the necessity of basting them during cooking.

I recommend following the packer's directions, because they fit the turkey you've purchased. When you buy a ready-stuffed turkey, it is very necessary to follow the directions.

A few markets in larger cities can provide fresh-killed turkeys to those who want them, especially at Thanksgiving time. But nowadays there's a premium on the fresh-killed bird. The bargains are to be found in turkeys fully prepared and fast-frozen while very fresh.

An overcooked turkey has dry meat; you want it tender, steaming, and *juicy!* So adjust the dinner to the turkey and don't set an inflexible hour for eating. Guests would rather wait longer and enjoy it more.

## TOMATO SLUSH

*1 can (46 ounces) vegetable juice cocktail or tomato juice*
*Juice and a little grated rind of 1 lemon*
*2 green onions, finely minced, with tops*
*3 or 4 minced parsley sprigs*
*Dash of pepper*
*Dash of Tabasco sauce*

Mix everything in a deep plastic container and freeze to a slush. This may take a little more than 2 hours. You can hurry it in ice cube trays.

Scoop into short, wide cocktail glasses.

You'll have enough left over to introduce another meal or to zip up your turkey bone soup, made from skin, scraps and, of course, the bones of the turkey.

## CORNBREAD

*1½ cups yellow cornmeal*
*1 cup flour*
*1 teaspoon salt*
*3 teaspoons baking powder*
*1 large egg*
*2 tablespoons bacon or ham drippings or melted margarine*
*1 cup milk*

This recipe is for two pans of cornbread: one pan to be broken up for the turkey stuffing; the other for the Bonus Recipe, page 39. The cornbread may be baked the night before the dinner or even earlier.

Measure cornmeal, flour, salt and baking powder into mixing bowl, stir to blend, and add egg, drippings or margarine and milk. Stir vigorously to mix smooth. Spread in two well-greased 9 × 9-inch baking pans. Bake at 425 F. for 15 to 20 minutes. Cool.

■ *Note: Cornbreads made from mixes, in fact most made not from mixes, are too sweet and crumbly. There's no sugar in this recipe, and only a small amount of shortening. Drippings add a great deal of flavor and provide a use for fat that too frequently is wasted.*

*In my opinion, most cornmeal is ground too fine. If you can find old fashioned, coarse-ground cornmeal (probably at a health food store), try it, if you don't mind the extra cost.*

## ROAST TURKEY WITH CORNBREAD STUFFING

In advance, thaw the frozen turkey, except a stuffed one, in which case follow package directions. This is best done in the refrigerator or a cool place, but the process can be hurried, if necessary, by placing the bird in the sink under cool, not hot, running water, in its plastic wrap, or by placing it in front of a fan. It is better to let it thaw naturally. Roasting an unstuffed turkey saves time, and now is recommended by authorities as a means of protection from food poisoning. Unfriendly bacteria develop well in the favorable medium of an enclosed stuffing kept warm, often for hours. If you do stuff the turkey, have both bird and stuffing cold, and stuff just before roasting.

## Turkey

Rinse turkey and wipe inside dry with paper toweling. Sprinkle interior with salt and pepper and place an onion and some celery leaves within. Rub skin with margarine if it's not a self-basting turkey. Roast, breast side up, at 325 F. in a shallow, open pan. Cover drumstick ends with foil and lay a loose sheet of foil over the bird for the last ½ hour in the oven.

Time for a 14-pounder, stuffed, is about 2½ hours; unstuffed, 2 hours. But follow the packer's guide, if directions are given. Time is variable. The bird I cooked took 2½ hours. I stuffed it, I must admit, this time. It's prettier! Test for doneness by pressing thigh, which should be soft or, better, check by thermometer inserted in the thickest part of the inside thigh muscle. Be careful not to touch the bone. Temperature should be 185 F.

## Stuffing Stock

While turkey roasts, simmer neck and giblets in water to cover with salt, a few peppercorns, the tails of the onions, a few sprigs of parsley and some celery tops. You'll use the stock to moisten the stuffing, and in the gravy. (Leftover gravy goes into turkey bone soup.)

Take the turkey liver from the stock as soon as it is tender. It cooks quickly. Cover with a little stock, and refrigerate for later uses.

## Stuffing

Combine stuffing ingredients, moisten with stuffing stock and place in buttered casserole to bake along with the turkey for the last 45 minutes. If you do stuff the turkey, your procedure obviously starts with preparing the stuffing or, first of all, cooking the giblets.

## Gravy

Take giblets from the stock, cut finely. Sauté mushrooms, sliced or chopped, to have them ready. Some-

## Turkey

*1 14–18-pound fresh or frozen, thawed turkey*
*1 small onion*
*Celery leaves*
*Margarine, if not a self-basting turkey*

## Stuffing Stock

*Turkey neck and giblets*
*Salt to taste*
*3 or 4 peppercorns*
*Tops of 1 bunch green onions (see Stuffing)*
*Sprigs of parsley*
*Celery tops*

## Stuffing

*1 pan baked cornbread (recipe preceding)*
*3 cups coarse crumbs of French bread*
*2 cups chopped celery*
*2 tablespoons minced parsley*
*1 teaspoon poultry seasoning or ½ teaspoon crumbled sage and ½ teaspoon poultry seasoning*
*1 bunch green onions with parts of tops, chopped*
*¼–½ pound cooked old-fashioned pork sausage, optional for added flavor*
*1 stick or ½ cup margarine, melted*
*Salt and pepper to taste*

## Gravy

*Some giblets (see recipe)*
*Mushrooms*

times I strain the giblet stock and thicken it with a
cornstarch paste, adding chopped giblets and mushrooms, so that the gravy base is ready when the turkey
comes out of the oven. Then it is a matter of adding
spoonfuls of drippings from the bird, tasting and ad-
justing seasonings. A great time saver.

■ *Note: Don't forget to allow 15 to 20 minutes after
roasting for the turkey to "set" for the carver's knife. It
will be much easier to slice if kept warm on its platter
for that much time.*

### MASHED RUTABAGAS, GREEN BEANS
Previously cooked, mashed rutabagas (yellow turnips)
may be reheated in a casserole or covered skillet on top
of the range. Green beans are best cooked at the very
last minute. Salt, pepper, melted margarine and, if you
want to add something, a tablespoonful of chopped or
slivered toasted almonds adds interest. But the almonds
aren't accounted for in the cost.

I personally would favor preparing the rutabagas
ahead, for the hard vegetable is something of a chore to
cut up and loses no flavor by being cooked and reheated the next day. Fresh green beans should be a last
minute thing; if you must compromise and use frozen
green beans, as I did, they're last minute, too.

### PINK GRAPEFRUIT AND AVOCADO SALAD WITH RADISH CHIPS

*Sections pink grapefruit*
*Avocado slices*
*Lettuce leaves*
*Sliced radishes*
*French dressing*

The salad is made by arranging sections of pink grapefruit and avocado slices attractively on crisp lettuce
leaves, centering the arrangement with a generous portion of very thinly sliced radishes. Your favorite dressing (preferably French!) will complete the picture.

### POACHED PEARS

*6 winter pears*
*½ cup sugar*
*1½ cups water*
*Juice and a little grated
peel of 1 lemon*

Pare pears, removing blossom end of each, but leaving
stems. Bring sugar, water, lemon juice and peel to boil,
simmer a few minutes, then drop in pears. Simmer
them, without crowding, until tender, turning frequently
in the syrup. I prefer a small, deep saucepan for this,
one that will accommodate two pears at a time; it is all
right to do the cooking in relays. Test pears with a cake
tester; don't overcook them. Fifteen minutes may be

about right, but it depends upon pear size. Transfer, as cooked, to deep glass dessert dishes, standing each pear upright. Cook syrup down a bit, pour over pears and serve at room temperature or chilled.

This pear dessert would take on more flavor if prepared early, and it isn't a troublesome process at all, if done ahead.

■ *Variations: Add 2 tablespoons of rum or brandy to the syrup. Or core the pears before poaching (they'll cook more quickly) and stuff them with macaroon crumbs later.*

*Drip chocolate sauce over them and sprinkle with slivered, toasted almonds. Or poach them in port or another sweet wine instead of the syrup.*

*A vanilla bean instead of lemon juice and peel might be cooked with the syrup. Or red cinnamon candy, or crushed peppermint sticks.*

*The flavor possibilities are many. Experiment for yourself!*

■ *Bonus Recipes*

## PLANTATION SHORTCAKE

For this bonus meal, cut the pan of cornbread into rectangles and lay over each a slice of ham, preferably Virginia, then slices of light and dark turkey meat. Cover with mushroom sauce made by adding sliced, sautéed mushrooms to standard white or cream sauce. Sprinkle with grated cheese and broil or bake at 375 F. until hot and bubbly. Serve with a salad.

*Cornbread (recipe page 36)*
*Sliced Virginia ham*
*Light and dark turkey meat*

### Sauce

*¼ pound mushrooms*
*White or cream sauce*
*(recipe page 19)*
*Grated cheese*

## TURKEY CURRY ON RICE

Melt butter in skillet or broad-based saucepan. Add onions, celery and apple and cook gently. Stir in curry powder, then flour. Add the stock gradually. Simmer gently to thicken sauce. Add turkey, salt and pepper to taste. Cook gently a few minutes and serve on rice.

Pass chutney, chopped peanuts, flaked coconut to sprinkle over the turkey. Other condiments, such as crumbled, crisp bacon, chopped hard-boiled egg, chopped green pepper, may be offered. Serves 4 to 6.

■ *Variations: Canned or fresh mushrooms may be cooked with the onions, celery and apple, if you wish.*

*¼ cup butter or margarine*
*4 to 5 green onions with tops, sliced*
*½ cup finely cut celery*
*1 apple, pared and diced*
*1 tablespoon curry powder (more or less, depending upon taste and strength of curry)*
*3 tablespoons flour*
*2 cups chicken or turkey stock or bouillon*
*2 cups diced cooked turkey*
*Salt, pepper to taste*

3 to 4 cups hot cooked rice
Chutney, chopped peanuts,
flaked coconut for garnish

¼ *cup or a little more of white wine could replace some of the stock.*

*If you have leftover ham in the refrigerator, up to half the turkey could be replaced by ham. This is a versatile leftover dish, adaptable to what you have on hand.*

### TURKEY AND NOODLES CASSEROLE

1 package (7 or 8 ounces)
egg noodles
1 onion, chopped
¼ green pepper, chopped
½ pound fresh mushrooms,
sliced or 1 cup canned
mushrooms
3 tablespoons butter or
margarine
1 can condensed tomato
soup
1 teaspoon salt
1 12-ounce can evaporated
milk
2 cups cooked diced turkey

Cook noodles in 2 quarts boiling, salted water until tender; drain. Sauté onion, green pepper and mushrooms in butter until tender but not browned. Add soup, salt, evaporated milk. Arrange noodles and turkey in layers in a casserole, pour soup mixture over them and bake 45 minutes at 350 F. Serves 6 to 8.

■ *Variation: If you have a cup of leftover, rather thick turkey gravy, you could use that instead of the tomato soup. A different color, a different flavor, but very good, too!*

# CAROL CUTLER

# A Low-Cost, Low-Cholesterol Party Menu

**MENU**

Fried Stuffed Mushroom Caps
Hot Pork Roll with Mustard Sauce
Baked Apple Compote
Coffee-Flavored Meringue with Chocolate Sauce
Glacéed Orange Sections

Total Cost of Dinner for 6: $13.61

Bonus Recipes: Candied Orange Peel
Chocolate-Covered Orange Peel
Orange Compote

Wines: Alsatian Riesling, California Chenin Blanc

*(Cost not included)*

Carol Cutler *has been a food columnist for the* Washington Post *and is a graduate of twelve years intensive training at the Cordon Bleu and l'Ecole des Trois Gourmands in Paris. She is the author of* Haute Cuisine for Your Heart's Deligh., A Low Cholesterol Cookbook for Gourmets.

othing about this menu makes one think of "diet" nor of low cost. From start to finish, this orchestration of flavors and unusual presentations turns the dollars spent for the food into an investment that should return handsome dividends in pleasing your guests.

Part of the secret is in giving a novel twist to what otherwise would be ordinary foods. In the first course, for example, pairs of mushroom caps are stuffed, breaded and deep fried. They are extravagant looking and tasting, but the cost is less than 85¢ a serving, including the crab meat used in the filling.

For the main course just two pounds of pork tenderloin is ground and mixed with other good flavors to satisfy six happy diners. Apples are served with the pork, but apples with a difference. They are sliced and baked and given a sharp, zesty flavor and some texture. This dish is a far cry from apple sauce. And the dessert blends two flavors that have a particular affinity for each other—coffee and chocolate.

But can a meal as glamorous as this be low in cholesterol, too? Again, from start to finish it will be an eye-opener to those who think that low-cholesterol cuisine has to be dull. For good heart health most doctors recommend that Americans, particularly American men, adopt more prudent eating habits and cut back on cholesterol-ladened fatty foods.

Pork was deliberately used in this menu to emphasize how much pork has changed over the years. The U.S. Dept. of Agriculture and the National Pork Producers Council point out that, through improved feeding and breeding, today's pork is 50 percent leaner than it was seventeen years ago. Thus, by using the loin eye or tenderloin of pork and trimming off the fat around it, you will be eating leaner meat than the heavily marbled pieces of beef that regularly appear on American tables. Pork loin has almost no marbling because all its fat is *around* it and easily removed.

It should be noted that a "chocolate" sauce is served with the dessert and that chocolate is an item to be avoided in low-cholesterol diets. Our sauce is made with cocoa, which is permitted. It is the fat in chocolate that is harmful. Cocoa has none, and in this recipe the fat is replaced with polyunsaturated margarine.

I hope this menu will demonstrate that just because the cook gives up fatty, artery-popping products, she or he does not have to give up delicious cuisine. Every original recipe that follows uses only products approved for low-cholesterol diets. The aim is to promote good heart health while pleasing the palate.

### FRIED STUFFED MUSHROOM CAPS

*2 shallots, finely chopped or 3 tablespoons chopped spring onions, white part only*
*¼ cup green pepper, finely chopped*
*½–1 cup clam juice*
*1 6½-ounce can crabmeat*
*½ cup grated low-fat cheese (also called "filled" cheese)*
*Juice of 1 lemon*
*½ cup bread crumbs for filling, plus extra for coating*
*Salt and pepper*
*24 mushroom caps, 1½–2 inches wide*
*Flour*
*2 egg whites, lightly beaten*
*Polyunsaturated oil for frying*
*Lemon wedges*
*Tartar sauce*

Put the shallots and green peppers in a small pot and pour in enough clam juice to cover them. Cover the pot and cook until they are tender. Scrape into a large bowl. Add the crabmeat, cheese, lemon juice and ½ cup of bread crumbs. Season well with salt and pepper, adding a little more clam juice if the filling seems too dry.

Fill two similar-sized mushroom caps with the filling, press the caps together and scrape off any excess filling that escapes. Repeat with the rest of the mushroom caps. Pour some flour in a dish, the egg whites in a second dish, and some breadcrumbs in a third dish. Dip the stuffed caps in the flour and coat well; pay particular attention to the center seam. Dip the caps in the egg whites, then into the bread crumbs. Coat the mushrooms well. Chill for at least 1 hour. If properly coated, the mushrooms will not separate during the frying, but if you worry about this, run a toothpick through the two caps and remove before serving.

Just before serving time, heat to medium hot 1 inch of oil in a large frying pan. Fry the stuffed mushrooms carefully, turning so that all sides will be a nice golden brown. Serve hot, garnished with lemon wedges and Tartar sauce.

■ *Note: The mushroom stems not used in the above recipe can be sliced and added to salads or chopped and sautéed to add to sauces. They can be added to a brown sauce to top hamburgers; chopped and fried with thinly sliced onions and refrigerated or frozen to keep for garnishing fried chops.*

*Any leftover clam juice can be frozen in its bottle*

since there will be enough room for expansion as it
freezes. Freezing does not change it at all.

Any yolks not used in low-cholesterol cooking can be
turned into delicious homemade mayonnaise. Since 2
egg yolks are forced to absorb almost 1½ cups of
beneficial polyunsaturated oil, doctors permit mayonnaise on a low-cholesterol diet.

## HOT PORK ROLL WITH MUSTARD SAUCE

Trim the pork of all visible fat and put the meat
through the finest blade of the grinder. Grind the ham.
Peel the onion and cut it into chunks. Peel the garlic
clove. Put the onion and garlic through the grinder,
then grind the pork and ham again. Put the margarine
through the grinder: it must be very cold or it cannot
be ground. Finally put the bread through the grinder.
The bread will push through all the food that was
ground before and also help bind the pork roll.

To the ground meat add the thyme, nutmeg, allspice, sage, oregano, salt and pepper. Mix very well
with your hands. Add the milk and the egg whites and
mix again. Fry a teaspoon of the meat and taste. Correct seasoning if necessary, then chill the meat.

While the meat is chilling, prepare the poaching
stock. In a fish poacher or other long pot, pour in water
to the ¾ level. Add the bones or cubes, bay leaf, carrot, salt and pepper. Bring the water to a simmer and
cook for 20 minutes.

Select a strong dish towel with no holes in it or use
2 layers of cheese cloth. Stretch the towel very flat.
Scoop the chilled meat onto the towel near one of the
long edges and pat the meat into a long roll, about 12
inches long and 4 inches wide. Roll the towel tightly
around the meat and tie the ends of the cloth tightly
with string. Poach the pork roll in the stock for 45
minutes, longer if the roll is thicker than 4 inches.

Lift the cooked roll from the stock and allow it to
drip for 5 minutes. Cut off the string and carefully un-
roll the meat. Cut the roll into slices and place them on
a warm serving platter. Spoon some of the mustard
sauce (recipe follows) over the top of the slices and
pass the rest of the sauce separately in a bowl. (This
pork roll is also delicious cold.)

*2 pounds pork tenderloin,
trimmed of all fat
¼ pound lean boiled ham
1 medium onion
1 garlic clove
8 tablespoons (1 stick)
polyunsaturated margarine,
from the freezer
2 slices white bread, with
crusts
½ teaspoon thyme
¼ teaspoon nutmeg
½ teaspoon allspice
¼ teaspoon sage
1 teaspoon oregano
1 tablespoon salt
1 teaspoon pepper
½ cup evaporated skimmed
milk
3 egg whites*

**For the stock:**

*Chicken or turkey bones or
4 chicken cubes
1 bay leaf
1 carrot
1 tablespoon salt
1 teaspoon pepper*

## MUSTARD SAUCE

**For ¾ cup sauce**

*1 teaspoon salt*
*2 tablespoons sugar*
*⅛ teaspoon pepper*
*2 teaspoons dry mustard*
*1 teaspoon cornstarch*
*½ cup frozen egg substitute*
*½ cup water*
*¼ cup vinegar*

In a small pot combine all the dry ingredients. Stir in the egg substitute, water and vinegar. Cook over medium heat, stirring often, until the sauce thickens; this will take about 3 minutes.

■ *Note: The tenderloin pork bones not used in the Hot Pork Roll can be added to any beans (lentils, navy, black-eyed, northern) as they are being cooked. The only other flavorings necessary are an onion studded with a clove, a bay leaf, a rib of celery and salt and pepper.*

## BAKED APPLE COMPOTE

*2 tablespoons polyun-*
*saturated margarine*
*3 pounds apples, preferably*
*Stayman, York or Rome*
*Rind of 1 lemon*
*3 teaspoons sugar*
*3 tablespoons whiskey or*
*bourbon*

Preheat oven to 325 F.

Smear the margarine in an 8-cup soufflé or similar baking dish. Peel the apples, quarter them, remove the cores and thinly slice.

With a swivel-bladed vegetable peeler remove the rind from the lemon and chop it finely. Put ⅓ of the apples in the baking dish, then sprinkle on ⅓ of the lemon peel, 1 teaspoon of sugar and 1 tablespoon of whiskey. Repeat two more times. Cover closely with aluminum foil and bake for 1½ hours.

■ *Note: In the above menu, two different recipes call for the same oven temperature: Baked Apple Compote and the Coffee-Flavored Meringue. Bake them together to save energy. At other times when slightly varying temperatures are called for, don't be too dogmatic about it; bake the different foods at the same time, but make adjustments in the timing.*

*After removing the rind from a lemon or an orange, wrap the fruit tightly in plastic wrap or aluminum foil to stop it from drying out.*

## COFFEE MERINGUE WITH CHOCOLATE SAUCE

*1½ cups sugar*
*½ cup water*
*6 egg whites*
*¼ teaspoon cream of tartar*
*1 teaspoon vanilla*
*2 tablespoons instant coffee,*
*plus 2 teaspoons*
*2 tablespoons corn starch*
*1 teaspoon polyunsaturated*
*oil*

Preheat oven to 325 F.

In a small pot boil the sugar and water to the soft-ball stage (238 F. on a candy thermometer). When the syrup reaches 100 F. on the thermometer, begin beating the egg whites with an electric beater. Sprinkle on the cream of tartar and beat the whites until very firm.

Pour the hot syrup over the beaten egg whites while continuing to beat at a fast speed. Turn the speed to high and beat for 2 minutes more. Add the vanilla and 2 tablespoons of instant coffee. Beat again at high speed until the flavorings are thoroughly blended in. Lightly fold in the corn starch.

Lightly oil an 8-cup soufflé mold and scoop the meringue into it. Tap the dish on the counter a few times to settle the meringue well into it. Smooth the top with a spatula and sprinkle 2 teaspoons of instant coffee over it.

Place the soufflé mold in a pan containing 1 inch of hot water. Place the pan in the oven and bake for 45 minutes to 1 hour, or until the meringue puffs and begins pulling away from the sides. Remove from the oven and cool. The meringue will shrink somewhat.

### CHOCOLATE SAUCE

Put all ingredients in the blender and blend for 1 minute. Pour the sauce in a small saucepan and bring to a slow simmer. Simmer for 1 minute. Serve the sauce hot with the coffee meringue.

*⅓ cup sugar*
*1 cup evaporated skimmed milk*
*3 tablespoons cocoa*
*5 tablespoons polyunsaturated margarine*
*1 teaspoon vanilla*
*2 tablespoons rum*
*1 tablespoon orange liqueur*

### RECYCLED ORANGES

With after-dinner coffee many hostesses like to serve candied ginger to nibble on. It is a nice, but extremely expensive touch. A more original and budget-minded tidbit can be easily substituted. It also happens to be a sweet that famous Maxim's in Paris serves with coffee —Glacéed Orange Sections. In the following set of recipes absolutely nothing is wasted—not the rind, not the water used for soaking the rind, not even the sugar syrup in which the rinds were cooked. See how three oranges kick off a series of budget-minded treats.

### GLACEED ORANGE SECTIONS

This is also the preliminary preparation for Candied Orange Peel (recipe follows).

Scrape away or cut off any dye stamps on the fruit. Carefully cut the rind of the oranges into four sections. Peel off the rind without tearing the orange membranes. Put the rind in a deep bowl, pour on 1 quart cold water and cover with a dish that just fits inside the bowl. The object of the dish is to keep the rinds submerged in the

*3 seedless naval oranges*
*1 quart water, plus 1 cup*
*3 cups sugar*
*1 tablespoon light corn syrup*
*Few drops orange food color (or few drops each red and yellow)*

water; without the weight they will float. Soak for at least 24 hours; keep in a cool spot, but not refrigerated.

Separate the orange sections and remove all the white pith, again being careful not to tear the membrane. Place on a wire rack and let stand overnight at room temperature. The fruit can also be dried in a slow oven (about 250 F.) for about a half hour, but the slow drying is better.

Prepare the sugar syrup by boiling together in a small pot 1 cup cold water, sugar, corn syrup and food color. Bring to a boil and cook almost to the hard crack stage (280 F. on a candy thermometer). Have a pan of cold water ready and, as soon as the syrup is finished, plunge the bottom of the syrup pan into the cold water to stop the cooking. If this is not done, the syrup will quickly turn sugary. Then place the syrup pot in a pan of hot water to keep it soft for dipping the oranges.

Have a lightly oiled cookie sheet ready. Carefully dip each orange section into the hot syrup, let it drip just a moment and place immediately on the cookie sheet. Work quickly, so the syrup will not harden. The orange sections can be held with kitchen tongs or a small fork. Let the glacéed oranges dry at least one hour.

■ *Note: These delicious orange morsels are generally served with coffee at the end of dinner and are best made the day they are to be served. The glacé process takes no more than 10 minutes. (Tangerines may also be used.)*

■ *Bonus Recipes*

### CANDIED ORANGE PEEL

*Rinds of 3 oranges*
*Water from preceding recipe*
*2½ cups sugar*

One piece at a time, lift the orange rind from the water and carefully scrape away all the white pith with a spoon, trying not to damage the skin. Use short strokes rather than long sweeps. Reserve the water in which the rind was soaked.

Put the rind in a pot and cover with fresh cold water. Bring to a boil and gently simmer for 1 hour. Drain.

Add the sugar to the reserved orange water, bring to a simmer and cook gently for 15 minutes. Add the rind, cover and cook very, very slowly for 4 hours. The syrup should barely bubble. Let the rind cool in the syrup. Makes about 1 pound.

■ *Note: Depending on how you intend to use the candied peel, it can be kept in a covered jar (for use on ice creams or chopped to mix with fruit desserts), drained and dried slowly in the oven (150 F. for 2 hours) for eating as a candy—it will have a slightly sharp flavor, in a way resembling candied ginger. Or drain and let dry at room temperature if it is to be coated with chocolate (recipe follows). Tightly covered and kept in the refrigerator, the candied orange rind, with or without syrup, will keep for at least six weeks.*

### CHOCOLATE-COVERED ORANGE PEEL

Cut the oven-dried candied orange peel in strips about ¼-inch wide. Melt chocolate with syrup over low heat. Dip orange strips into the hot chocolate and place on waxed paper. Do not let orange pieces touch. Dry at least three hours; keep in cool place.

*8 ounces semisweet chocolate*
*¼ cup orange syrup (reserved from preceding recipe)*
*1 pound candied orange peel*

### ORANGE COMPOTE

Remove just the rind (none of the white part) from 3 or 4 of the oranges in long strips—a potato peeler works fine. Cut the rind into very, very thin julienne strips. Meanwhile bring syrup and water to a boil, add rind, cover partially and simmer for 15 minutes.

*6 seedless oranges*
*2 cups syrup from preceding recipe*
*1 cup water*
*½ cup orange liqueur*

Remove rind and white part from all six oranges and cut in even ¼-inch slices. Place the slices in a deep bowl that can withstand boiling syrup. Pour the hot syrup and rind over the orange slices. Immediately pour in the liqueur. Cover closely at once, let cool to room temperature, then refrigerate for at least three hours.

For serving, transfer orange slices to a deep serving bowl, spoon on some of the syrup and heap the rind on top. The rind is soft and sweet and meant to be eaten.

■ *Note: Any leftover syrup may be frozen and used whenever you need a fruity sugar syrup for dessert-making.*

## JULIE DANNENBAUM

# An Elegant Fish Menu for Springtime

**MENU**

Warm Asparagus Vinaigrette
Stuffed Baked Fish with Sautéed Shrimp and Mushrooms
Braised Celery
Angel Food Roulade

Total Cost of Dinner for 6: $16.00

Bonus Recipe: Asparagus Soup

Wine: California Chablis
*(Cost not included)*

Julie Dannenbaum *is the founding director of the largest nonprofessional cooking school in the United States, the Creative Cooking School in Philadelphia, Pennsylvania. She is the author of* Julie Dannenbaum's Creative Cooking School *and* Menus for All Occasions.

ining should always be one of life's greatest pleasures under *any* circumstances. Nothing is more frustrating than not having enough money to spend, especially on food. It has always been pleasurable for me to entertain lavishly, but to dine with five or six friends inexpensively can be an exciting challenge.

For me, the key to cutting the food budget is utilizing those foods which are in season; I really do not enjoy strawberries in January or rhubarb in December. Luscious ripe peaches and tender corn on the cob are taste thrills I look forward to each summer, just as the first fresh shad roe in spring. The menu I've selected makes use of these foods which are in season.

It is my opinion that when we are all watching our food budget, that now and again we should insert a minor touch of extravagance into our menus, such as a little heavy cream, a few spoonfuls of cognac, a piece of truffle or perhaps a few shrimp, as I have placed in the following menu.

## WARM ASPARAGUS VINAIGRETTE

Take 2½ pounds medium-sized asparagus and break or cut off tough ends. Peel with a potato peeler or use a small knife. Lay the asparagus in a skillet and add cold water halfway to its depth. Add 1 teaspoon salt. Do not cover.

Bring to a boil, turn burner to a simmer and cook 8 to 10 minutes. Asparagus should be tender crisp. Drain and dry on a kitchen towel. Place in an oval serving dish.

Serve warm with vinaigrette dressing.

*2½ pounds medium-sized asparagus*
*1 teaspoon salt*

### The Dressing

Into a small bowl put 1 teaspoon salt, ½ teaspoon freshly ground black pepper, 1 egg yolk and 1 teaspoon Dijon mustard. Mix with fork until sticky. Add ¼ cup red wine vinegar and ¾ cup oil. Mix well and pour over asparagus while warm.

**The Dressing**

*1 teaspoon salt*
*½ teaspoon freshly ground black pepper*
*1 egg yolk*
*1 teaspoon Dijon mustard*
*¼ cup red wine vinegar*
*¾ cup vegetable, peanut or olive oil*

■ *Note: Save asparagus water, trimmings and stems for soup.*

## STUFFED BAKED FISH WITH SAUTEED SHRIMP AND MUSHROOMS

### The Fish

*4–6 pound whole fish,
including head and tail
Juice of ½ lemon, plus
4 tablespoons
1 teaspoon salt
½ teaspoon freshly ground
black pepper
4 tablespoons melted butter*

### The Fish

Select a fish weighing 4 to 6 pounds, count ¾ pound per person. Almost any fish can be used although I do not recommend using flounder or fluke as they are dry and mildly flavored. Leave head and tail on fish. Clean the fish and remove the backbone, leaving the fish open from its head to tail, on the abdomen side, or have fishmonger do it. Save bones and all trimmings for stock.

Wash and dry fish thoroughly. Sprinkle inside of fish cavity with juice of ½ lemon, 1 teaspoon salt and ½ teaspoon freshly ground black pepper. Fill loosely with the following stuffing.

### The Stuffing

*1 loaf unsliced bread for
breadcrumbs
4 tablespoons butter
½ cup finely chopped
scallions, white part only
1 cup cooked frozen
spinach, or fresh
2 egg yolks, beaten
⅛ teaspoon freshly grated
nutmeg
1 teaspoon salt
½ teaspoon freshly ground
black pepper
½ cup lemon juice*

### For Garnish

*Lemon quarters
Watercress
½ pound each large
mushrooms and medium-
sized shrimp, sautéed*

### The Stuffing

To prepare breadcrumbs for stuffing, cut off top of loaf (one-inch) and scoop out interior of bread, leaving a wall of bread ½-inch thick, forming a box shape, or croustade. Put bread from center in chunks into a blender or food processor to make crumbs.

Melt 4 tablespoons butter in a pan and when hot add ½ cup finely chopped scallions (white part only) and cook while stirring, 3 or 4 minutes. Add 1 cup (one 10-ounce package frozen cooked spinach—cooked according to package directions) drained, squeezed and finely chopped. (Fresh spinach may be used.) Cook the spinach a few minutes and add the breadcrumbs. Mix all ingredients together and remove from fire.

Add 2 egg yolks, beaten. Season with ⅛ teaspoon freshly grated nutmeg, 1 teaspoon salt, ½ teaspoon freshly ground black pepper. Add ½ cup lemon juice to moisten mixture. Pack loosely into fish and either sew or skewer the opening.

Place fish belly down on a buttered ovenproof dish and brush with 4 tablespoons each melted butter and lemon juice. Bake 10 minutes per pound at 375 F. Baste with pan juices twice during baking time. Serve directly from baking dish garnished with fresh lemon quarters nestled in a bunch of watercress.

Surround fish with Sautéed Mushrooms and Shrimp.

## SAUTÉED MUSHROOMS AND SHRIMP

Take ½ pound large mushrooms. Wipe dry with a damp cloth. Remove stems even with cap. Cut them into quarters. Remove shells from ½ pound medium-sized shrimp and melt 4 tablespoons butter in a skillet. When butter is hot, add the mushrooms and shrimp, ½ teaspoon salt and ½ teaspoon freshly ground pepper and 1 tablespoon lemon juice. Toss over high flame for 3 to 4 minutes. Do not overcook. Place around fish and sprinkle with 1 tablespoon finely chopped dill.

½ pound large mushrooms
½ pound medium-sized shrimp
4 tablespoons butter
½ teaspoon salt
½ teaspoon freshly ground black pepper
1 tablespoon lemon juice
1 tablespoon finely chopped dill

■ *Note: Reserve fish bones and trimmings and shrimp shells for fish stock.*
*Croustade can be brushed with butter and baked and used as a container for scrambled eggs.*
*Save mushroom stems for duxelles or soup.*

## BRAISED CELERY

Select three heads of celery. Trim away outer ribs and leaves and reserve for use in a later recipe. Trim root ends neatly. Wash, dry and cut lengthwise. You now have 6 pieces.
Put celery into pot and cover with cold water. Bring to a boil and cook 5 minutes. Drain. In an ovenproof dish, scatter ¼ cup finely diced bacon, ¼ cup finely chopped shallots, and ¼ cup finely chopped carrot. Lay celery on top of mixture and sprinkle with 1 teaspoon salt and 1 teaspoon freshly ground white pepper. Pour over 1 cup of chicken or veal stock and bring to boil on top of stove.
Cover the dish with lid and place in 350 F. oven for 1 hour. Sprinkle with 1 tablespoon finely chopped parsley before serving.

3 heads celery
¼ cup finely diced bacon
¼ cup finely chopped shallots
¼ cup finely chopped carrot
1 teaspoon salt
1 teaspoon freshly ground white pepper
1 cup chicken or veal stock
1 tablespoon finely chopped parsley

■ *Note: Save celery tops for soup, stock or fritters.*

## ANGEL FOOD ROULADE *

### The Cake

Line an 11 x 17 x 1-inch baking sheet pan with baking parchment. Do not grease.
Mix together ¼ cup granulated sugar, ¼ teaspoon salt and ¾ cup cake flour. Beat in a mixer or whip by hand ¾ cup of egg whites. When foamy, add ¼ tea-

**The Cake**
¼ cup granulated sugar, plus ½ cup
¼ teaspoon salt
¾ cup cake flour
¾ cup egg whites

* *Roulade is a French word for roll.*

*¼ teaspoon cream of tartar*
*1 cup evaporated milk*
*1 teaspoon almond extract*
*2 tablespoons confectioner's*
*sugar, sifted*

spoon cream of tartar. Continue to beat until soft peaks form. Do not overbeat the whites. Beat in 1 teaspoon almond extract. Beat in 1 tablespoon at a time ½ cup sugar until mixture is glossy. Fold in gently the sugar, salt and cake flour mixture.

Pour batter onto the prepared baking sheet and place in a 350 F. oven for 20 to 25 minutes. Let cake cool to room temperature in pan. Turn out onto wax paper, dusted with 2 tablespoons sifted confectioner's sugar. Spread with the following filling.

## The Filling

*2 cups strawberries ** 
*1 egg white, slightly beaten*
*Granulated sugar for*
*coating berries*
*2–3 tablespoons con-*
*fectioner's sugar*
*1–2 tablespoons kirsch*
*1½ cups thick sour cream*

** Reserve 6 of largest*
*strawberries with stems for*
*garnish.*

## The Filling

Take 2 cups strawberries, reserving six of the largest and prettiest. Do not remove stems of these six. Dip them into 1 egg white, slightly beaten, and roll them in granulated sugar. Set aside.

Slice remainder of berries and sweeten with 2 or 3 tablespoons confectioner's sugar. Add 1 or 2 tablespoons kirsch and stir into 1½ cups thick sour cream. Spread on roulade and roll up from the wide side. Place on long narrow serving dish and lay the 6 whole strawberries down the center.

■ *Note: Save yolks for Hollandaise and Bearnaise sauces, crème caramel or sponge cake, or zabaglione.*

■ *Bonus Recipe*
## ASPARAGUS SOUP

*4 tablespoons butter*
*1 onion*
*1 potato*
*2 cups reserved asparagus*
*ends and trimmings*
*Reserved asparagus water*
*3 cups light cream or milk*
*1 cup chicken stock*
*1 teaspoon salt*
*½ teaspoon freshly ground*
*white pepper*
*Parsley, chives or scallion*
*tops*

Melt 3 tablespoons butter in a pan. Add 1 onion, finely chopped and cook, while stirring, 3 minutes. Add 1 potato, washed, peeled, and diced. Add the reserved asparagus ends and trimmings; there should be about 2 cups. Add the reserved asparagus water, 2 cups light cream or milk, and 1 cup of chicken stock. Bring to a boil, turn to a simmer and cook about 15 to 20 min. Season with 1 teaspoon salt and ½ teaspoon freshly ground white pepper and purée mixture in food processor, blender or food mill. Thin with 1 cup heated light cream, chicken stock or heavy cream, according to budget. Before serving, add 1 tablespoon soft butter and dust each serving with 1 teaspoon finely chopped parsley, chives or scallion tops. Serves 6.

# TRAVERS MONCURE EVANS

# A Half a Ham Serves 6 More Than Once

**MENU**

Chilled Pumpkin Soup
Filets of Ham with Chutney Butter
Green Beans and Water Chestnuts
Spoon Bread Soufflé
Tropical Sherbet

Total Cost of Dinner for 6: $15.15

Bonus Recipes: Ham and Lentils, Ham Kebabs

Wine: Beaujolais
*(Cost not included)*

Travers Moncure Evans *is a former advertising copywriter who, with David Greene, authored* The Meat Book: A Consumer's Guide to Selecting, Buying, Cutting, Storing, Freezing and Carving. *She served on the editorial committee for* New York Entertains, *Doubleday & Co., and lives in New York.*

his menu suggests a way for you to cut yourself in for a big, delicious bargain—plus bonus meals—by purchasing a large cut of meat. Purchasing large cuts and dividing them into several separate meals is usually an economical way to shop. If you can divide the large cuts up yourself without the assistance of a butcher, there are even greater savings to be had.

For instance, in this case we purchased a half, semi-boneless, fully-cooked, 6-pound ham and cut it into the filets. Purchased separately, the same precut kind of ham steaks can cost as much as 50¢ more per pound than those that we cut—yet this do-it-yourself job couldn't be easier.

To prepare your own filets, all you need is a very sharp, thin-bladed knife. Simply put down the ham with *surface containing the bone up.* You will notice that one side of the ham contains bone and the other is boneless. Grasp the boneless side in one hand and with the other hand insert the knife as closely as possible to the bone. Slice down as near to the bone as you can until the bony side of the ham falls away.

To cut the filets, place the boneless piece of ham down on its freshly cut surface and slice from the top vertically into six ¼–½-inch pieces. These filets provide the meat for our menu—but there are still 2 to 2½ pounds of ham and a bone remaining as the basis for several other meals. Well-covered in the refrigerator, the remaining ham will keep nicely for up to a week and provide omelettes and casseroles if diced—or skewered ham kebabs if cut into chunks. And with that bone and any remaining scraps—how about a pot of pea soup?

## CHILLED PUMPKIN SOUP

Melt butter in heavy saucepan. Chop onion coarsely and sauté in melted butter until soft. Add stock and pumpkin, stirring until blended. Bring to a boil, then lower the heat and simmer for five minutes. Purée the hot pumpkin mixture in a blender or food mill, then pour through a fine sieve into a large bowl. Add salt and pepper, sugar, allspice, mace and nutmeg, then chill. Before serving, thin with light cream to the con-

*2 tablespoons butter*
*1 small onion*
*2½ cups chicken stock*
*1 29-ounce can pumpkin (unsweetened) or 2 cups puréed, cooked pumpkin*
*Salt to taste*
*Freshly ground black pepper to taste*
*½ teaspoon sugar*

½ teaspoon allspice
¼ teaspoon mace
¼ teaspoon nutmeg
Light cream
Freshly grated nutmeg


1 stick (½ cup) unsalted
butter, softened
¼ cup chutney, finely
chopped
6 filets of ham

sistency desired and, if necessary, adjust seasonings. Garnish each serving with freshly grated nutmeg.

## FILETS OF HAM WITH CHUTNEY BUTTER

Preheat broiler.

Cream the softened butter together with finely chopped chutney. Divide the butter equally among the 6 filets of ham. Spread evenly over each filet and arrange the filets on a flame-proof baking dish. Place under broiler about 5 inches from the source of heat and cook for about 8 to 10 minutes or until the ham is heated through and is slightly glazed. Serve immediately.

■ *Note: If you wish to heat the filets in the same oven as the spoon bread (recipe below), bake in a 400 F. oven for approximately 20 minutes. However, the ham will not have the attractive glaze that broiled ham has.*

## GREEN BEANS AND WATER CHESTNUTS

1½ pounds fresh green
beans
2 tablespoons butter
1 can water chestnuts,
drained and coarsely
chopped
1 tablespoon soy sauce
Salt and freshly ground
black pepper to taste

Trim green beans and cut them diagonally into 1½-inch lengths. Plunge them into a large pot of briskly boiling water and cook for about 5 minutes—or until they are cooked but still crunchy. Immediately pour the beans into a colander and hold under cold running water to stop cooking. Before serving, melt butter in a heavy saucepan and add beans and water chestnuts. Toss with the soy sauce, and heat thoroughly. Season to taste with salt and pepper. Serve immediately.

## SPOON BREAD SOUFFLÉ

4 cups milk
1 cup corn meal
2 tablespoons butter
½ teaspoon salt
4 eggs, separated

Preheat the oven to 400 F. Grease a 2-quart casserole or soufflé dish.

In a bowl, blend 1 cup of milk with the corn meal. Scald the remaining 3 cups of milk in the top of a double boiler. Add the corn meal mixture to the scalded milk and stir constantly over simmering water for ten minutes. Add butter and salt and remove from heat.

Beat egg yolks briefly. Beat egg whites until stiff. Fold yolks and whites into corn meal mixture. Pour mixture into prepared casserole. Bake for 45 minutes. Serve immediately with softened butter if desired.

## TROPICAL SHERBET

Add confectioner's sugar to drained pineapple and stir until sugar is dissolved. Combine pineapple mixture with the banana purée, orange and lemon juices, and chill until not quite firm.

Beat the egg whites until stiff and fold gradually into the nearly frozen fruit mixture. Beat mixture until light and fluffy. Divide the tropical sherbet among 6 parfait glasses, place on a rack in a freezer and freeze until firm. Remove from freezer about 10 minutes before serving. Garnish each serving with a sprig of mint or a slice of banana if desired.

*¾ cup confectioner's sugar*
*1½ cups canned, crushed pineapple, drained*
*3 large bananas, puréed in a blender*
*½ cup fresh orange juice*
*⅓ cup fresh lemon juice*
*2 egg whites*
*Sprigs of mint or 6 banana slices (optional)*

## ■ *Bonus Recipes*

## HAM AND LENTILS

Soak lentils in cold water for 2 hours. Drain and set aside. Sauté onion in butter or margarine until soft but not brown. Add the water, stock or beer, the ham bone and scraps, and the drained lentils. Cover and simmer for 3 hours. Add more water if the mixture gets dry. Before serving remove the bone and add vinegar, lemon zest, salt and freshly ground pepper to taste. Serve as a main course with a green salad.

*1 pound dried lentils*
*1 onion, chopped*
*2 tablespoons butter or margarine*
*1 cup water, stock or beer*
*Ham bone and scraps*
*1 tablespoon vinegar*
*Grated zest of 1 lemon*
*Salt and freshly ground black pepper*

## HAM KEBABS

Alternate chunks of ham with chunks of pineapple on skewers. Heat under broiler for approximately 15 minutes. Serve with rice.

*Ham chunks cut from left-over ham*
*Fresh or canned pineapple chunks*

# EDWARD GIOBBI

# An Italian Menu

**MENU**

Fish Soup
Sausages with Beans
Ricotta Balls

Total Cost of Dinner for 6: $5.28

Bonus Recipe: Sausages with Cauliflower

Wine: Segesta * Red
*(Cost not included)*

Edward Giobbi, *a painter of international reputation, is a passionate devotee of fine food and wine. Author of* Italian Family Cooking, *Mr. Giobbi raises his own fruits and vegetables and is known throughout the culinary world as a master Italian cook.*

* *Segesta wine can be purchased in gallons or half gallons and is one of the most reasonable imported wines.*

here are many ways to cook nourishing, tasty dishes at very reasonable prices. The following is just one example of how to serve an interesting menu at a very reasonable price.

The variations are endless. The sausage recipe is one example of how much one can save by simply taking the trouble to prepare the sausages oneself. The results will be a tastier sausage, a leaner sausage, a fresher sausage, not to mention a cheaper sausage.

Often, when we entertain and serve sausages, we cook the sausages several different ways: sausages with beans, and sausages with cauliflower, for instance. This recipe is especially good for large groups because it gives your guests a choice.

Please note that there should be enough money left over for wine, bread and a nice tossed salad if desired.

Fresh seasonal fruit is the best dessert and fresh sliced peaches served in white or red wine (served in a wine glass) are divine.

## FISH SOUP
### Brodo di Pesce

This soup can be made for practically nothing. Fish heads are available in fish stores and in many cases your fishmonger will give them to you free of charge.

To clean the fish heads remove the gills with a sharp knife or scissors—wash the heads thoroughly, drain them and set aside.

Sauté onions in olive oil. When onions wilt, add garlic and tomatoes. Cook over high heat, stirring constantly for several minutes; add parsley and fennel. Cover and cook over medium heat for about 5 minutes and add water, celery, carrot, bay leaf, salt and fish heads. Bring to a gentle boil with the cover partially off for about 30 minutes.

When soup is cooled, strain the broth and set aside. Remove edible flesh from fish heads such as cheeks and flesh behind head, discarding bones, etc., and add to broth.

Fifteen minutes before broth is to be served add rice. Stir occasionally and when rice is firm to the teeth, mix in optional ½ cup grated cheese. Serve hot.

*Fresh fish heads, cleaned and washed*
*3 tablespoons olive oil*
*1 medium onion, chopped*
*2 cloves garlic, chopped*
*1 cup tomatoes*
*2 tablespoons chopped parsley*
*(Italian, if possible)*
*1 teaspoon fennel (either fresh or seeds—½ cup if fresh)*
*1½ quarts water*
*1 rib celery*
*1 carrot*
*1 bay leaf*
*Salt*
*¾ cup rice*
*½ cup grated Pecorino Romano, Sardo or Parmigiano cheese (optional)*

■ *Note: If the occasion arises and a large fresh fish head is given to you, make the stock, strain and freeze the soup. It freezes very well and is excellent as a stock in risotto, etc.*

■ *Variations: Use croutons instead of grated cheese. Dice 6 thin slices of white bread in squares about ½-inch square. Cut 2 large cloves garlic in slivers and sauté in a large skillet in 4 tablespoons of olive oil (or butter or margarine). When the garlic browns, discard. Sauté the bread squares in the hot oil until a golden brown. Serve with the hot soup at the table so that each guest can add the croutons to his bowl.*

*For a heartier soup add ½ bunch of fresh broccoli (cleaned, washed and cut in 1-inch pieces) when the rice is added to the broth. To clean broccoli, skin the stem, quarter and cut into 1-inch pieces. Skin the stems of the florets. If cleaned properly, the stems are very sweet and tasty.*

## A NOTE ABOUT SAUSAGE MAKING

You can save about 50¢ per pound if you go to the trouble to make your own sausages. The average pork butt (Boston Butt) weighs about 4½ pounds, boned it weighs about 4¼ pounds. It costs about 95¢ per pound, if you make the sausages yourself. The average price of Italian sausages in the supermarket is $1.45 per pound.

### For 3 pounds of sausages

*2–4 strands of pork casings ***
*3 lbs. boneless pork butt †*
*1¾ teaspoons salt*
*2 tablespoons freshly ground black pepper*
*2½ teaspoons crushed fennel seeds (optional)*

*\* Pork casings can be purchased in most Italian meat stores. Casings are salted and can be kept in the refrigerator for several months.*
*† Pork butt is usually purchased whole. Have butcher remove flat bone or remove bone yourself and save for sauces.*

Rinse pork casings and let soak in lukewarm water for 1 hour or more. Rinse and drain.

Remove excess fat from pork and set aside (not more than ½ inch should be left on outside of butt). Either thinly slice the meat and with a sharp knife coarsely chop it by hand (this method is preferable) or coarsely grind the meat. Save bone for stews, sauces, etc.

Blend meat with salt, pepper and fennel seeds. Stuff one casing at a time. To do this, slip one end of the casing over the mouth of a sausage funnel with a wide spout * or use a regular sausage stuffer. Tie the end of the casing with a string. Stuff about 1 teaspoon of

*\* Sausage funnels with wide spouts can usually be purchased in Italian stores or use a regular sausage stuffer.*

pork into the funnel so that about ½ inch of it pro-trudes from the end of the spout like the tip of a finger, then work the casing up the outside of the spout. The pork protruding from the end of the spout will help the casing slide up easier.

When the tied end of the casing reaches the tip of the spout, begin stuffing the meat into the funnel by holding the funnel by the spout in one hand and stuffing the ground pork into the spout, forcing the meat to the end of the spout with the thumb. Allow the filled casing to slip gradually as it is stuffed. If links are desired, tie off sausage about every three inches. If the casing breaks (which usually happens) tie off both sides of break and continue as before.

## SAUSAGE II

For an unusually tasty sausage try this recipe. Use same ingredients as in preceding recipe, but eliminate the fennel seed and add ingredients at right.

Mix all ingredients together, stuff in pork casings, same as in pork sausage recipe.

*¾ pound coarsely ground butt (or other ground pork)*
*½ cup chopped provolone cheese **
*3 tablespoons chopped parsley (Italian if possible)*
*½ cup dry white wine*
*1 teaspoon crushed black pepper*
*1 teaspoon salt*
*1 tablespoon finely chopped garlic*

*\* Use any mild cheese such as Swiss if provolone is not available.*

## SAUSAGES WITH BEANS *
### Salsicce con Fagioli

**The Sausages**

Sauté sausages, uncovered, in oil, over low heat. As fat in sausages begins to melt, raise heat to moderate, prick sausages to allow fat to escape and turn sausages oc-casionally. Cook until sausages are brown.

After sausages are brown, pour off most of fat, leav-ing about 1 tablespoon, or as much as desired. (I personally prefer to pour off all of the fat and add 2 tablespoons of olive oil.)

Add wine, cover and lower heat. Cook until the wine cooks out. Set aside and keep warm.

*8 sausage links or 1½ pounds*
*2 tablespoons olive oil*
*½ cup dry white wine (optional)*

### The Beans

Preheat oven to 375 F. In an ovenproof casserole sauté onions and celery in olive oil (sausage drippings may

*1½ cups chopped onions*
*1 cup chopped celery*

3 tablespoons olive oil
1 teaspoon rosemary
1 bay leaf
1 teaspoon chopped garlic
1 cup strained tomatoes
1 can of cannellini beans,
drained, or 1 cup of dried
white beans soaked over-
night and cooked in water
until tender
Salt and freshly ground
black pepper


3 eggs
2 tablespoons sugar
1 pound ricotta
1 cup flour
5 teaspoons baking powder
¾ teaspoon salt
2 teaspoons brandy or
bourbon
Corn, peanut oil or
vegetable shortening
Powdered sugar


1½ pounds sausages
1 cauliflower, cut in
flowerets
2 tablespoons olive oil
1 cup sliced onions
½ teaspoon dried rosemary
1 teaspoon minced garlic
2 tablespoons chopped
parsley
½ teaspoon hot pepper
flakes
½ cup wine vinegar
1 tablespoon tomato paste
½ cup tomatoes

be used instead). Cover and simmer for about 10 minutes or until onion wilts. Add herbs and tomatoes,
beans, salt and pepper. Cook covered about 10 minutes.
In the meantime cut sausages in 1-inch lengths, add
sausages and reserved pan juices. Cover and bake 30
minutes. Serve hot.

### RICOTTA BALLS
#### Palline di Ricotta

Mix all ingredients together except oil and powdered
sugar, cover and let rest for 1 hour. Put about 1½ to
2 inches of oil in a small skillet. Heat the oil until it is
quite hot. Then drop 1 teaspoon of batter at a time
into the skillet. The oil should boil violently when
batter is added. Cook several minutes until the balls
are golden brown. Remove with slotted spoon, blot on
paper towels and dust with powdered sugar. Yield: 48
to 50 balls.

■ *Note: I have tested this recipe with cottage cheese
instead of the ricotta and it works!*

■ *Bonus Recipe*
### SAUSAGES WITH CAULIFLOWER
#### Salsicce Alla Marchigiana

Sauté sausages in a skillet over low heat. As sausages
begin to release fat, prick the sausages and cook over
moderate heat uncovered until sausages are brown. In
the meantime, blanch cauliflower in boiling water,
drain and set aside. Discard all but about 1 tablespoon
of fat. Add olive oil, cauliflower and onions. Cook
until onions wilt. Add rosemary, garlic, parsley, hot
pepper flakes, wine vinegar and tomato paste. Salt to
taste. Cover and cook over moderate heat, mixing
often. When vinegar cooks out, add tomatoes and cook
uncovered over moderate heat for about 10 minutes.

■ *Note: Do not overcook cauliflower during the blanch-
ing process.*

## CAROL GUBER

# A Mid-East Lamb Feast

**MENU**

Zucchini Stuffed with Spinach
Skewered Lamb and Eggplant
Rice Pilaf
Caramel Custard with Bananas and Raisins

Total cost of dinner for 6: $16.75

Bonus Recipe: Spinach Rolls in Pastry

Carol Guber *is a talented newcomer to the cooking field. Following worldwide travels as a freelance photographer, she returned to New York to start Guber-Lalli Assoc., a service which caters private and corporate events. She has been the producer and star of a weekly television series on WSNL TV, "Long Island Tonight."*

hough Middle Eastern in tone, this menu has a general appeal that should suit the fussiest eater. It can be prepared in a short amount of time, employs a number of inexpensive ingredients, and provides leftovers for later meals. Following are some tips you should keep in mind when planning and preparing this menu:

■ Shoulder is one of the cheapest cuts of lamb and you don't have to be too particular about the quality in order to make the main course (Skewered Lamb and Eggplant) successfully. The ground meat is combined with bread crumbs, which can be made from stale bread. Grind stale bread in the blender and you will never have to spend money for bread crumbs again! Any leftover bits of raw meat, such as the ground lamb, hamburger, or pork, can be placed in a plastic bag, put in the freezer, and used later.

■ The skewered lamb is served on rice pilaf, and any leftovers will make a novel cold rice salad.

■ When buying vegetables such as eggplant, zucchini and spinach used in this menu, try shopping late on Saturday. Often the greengrocer will discount more perishable items to avoid keeping them over the weekend. Saturdays are an excellent time to buy vegetables for stew or soup. But for these recipes, just make sure the vegetables are still firm—a few bruises in the eggplant can easily be cut out.

■ In addition to spinach, the zucchini recipe calls for mushroom stems. Save the caps for a recipe that needs them whole—or they can be added onto the skewers for our main course.

■ Any extra spinach stuffing can be used as a filling for crêpes and topped with Mornay sauce. We have provided a Bonus Recipe for the mixture, Spinach Rolls in Pastry. It requires philo or strudel dough, available at gourmet markets or Greek or Hungarian shops. The dough isn't very expensive but looks elegant. The thin sheets are folded into triangles around the stuffing, then baked and served as flaky appetizers. Other leftovers can also be used as a stuffing such as our lamb balls or a seafood combination.

■ The dessert is a simple variation on the classic Caramel Custard. You can substitute seasonal fruit such as apples or berries.

In all these recipes the object is to create an entertaining meal and save money at the same time.

### ZUCCHINI STUFFED WITH SPINACH

*1 pound fresh spinach*
*1 small onion, chopped*
*3 tablespoons unsalted butter*
*¼ pound mushroom stems, chopped*
*1 teaspoon dill*
*½ teaspoon Tabasco sauce*
*Salt and pepper to taste*
*¼ cup fresh bread crumbs*
*6 small zucchini*
*¼ cup mozzarella cheese, grated*

Preheat over to 350 F.
Steam spinach until slightly wilted.
Sauté onions in butter until clear and add chopped mushroom stems, dill, Tabasco sauce, salt, pepper and spinach. When mixture is combined, add enough bread crumbs to bind. Correct the seasonings.
Clean the zucchini and slice in half lengthwise. Scrape out seeds and cook in salted water about 15 minutes. Keep firm.
Spread spinach mixture into zucchini shells and sprinkle with mozzarella. Place in buttered baking dish and bake for 15 minutes or until tender.

### SKEWERED LAMB AND EGGPLANT

*1 medium-sized eggplant*
*Salt to taste*
*1½ pounds lamb shoulder, ground*
*1 tablespoon lemon juice*
*¼ cup bread crumbs*
*½ teaspoon mint leaves*
*1 egg, beaten*
*Salt and pepper to taste*
*2 cups plain yogurt*
*1 tablespoon turmeric*

Skin eggplant and cut into 1-inch cubes. Sprinkle with salt and allow to stand for 1 hour.
Combine ground lamb, lemon juice, bread crumbs, mint leaves, egg, salt and pepper. Form into balls about an inch in diameter.
Place lamb balls in a pan, only one deep, and pour half the yogurt mixed with turmeric over the lamb.
Drain the eggplant and toss in remaining yogurt mixture. Separately marinate both the eggplant and lamb for at least two hours.
On skewers alternate the lamb, eggplant and optional mushrooms caps. Place under broiler for about 20 minutes—about 10 minutes each side. The lamb should still be juicy.
Serve with Rice Pilaf (recipe follows).

### RICE PILAF

*½ cup butter*
*1 medium onion, chopped*
*2 cups uncooked white rice*
*3 cups chicken stock*
*½ teaspoon salt*
*2 cups water*
*¼ cup pine nuts*
*Chopped parsley*

Melt butter in a skillet, sauté the onion until clear and add the rice. Cook until all the butter is absorbed.
Add the chicken stock, salt and water. Cover and cook for 30 minutes or until all of the water is absorbed.
Toss with pine nuts and parsley. Serve hot.

## CARAMEL CUSTARD
## WITH BANANAS AND RAISINS

Preheat oven to 350 F.

To caramelize mold, heat ½ cup sugar and water in a 6-cup mold and swirl to cover sides and bottom. Take off of heat and place sliced bananas on bottom. Sprinkle with raisins. Place immediately into a pan of cold water to set mold.

Lightly beat the whole eggs and egg yolks together with ¾ cup sugar using a wire whisk.

Heat the milk until warm but not boiling. Slowly pour into egg mixture in an even stream while continuing to beat mixture.

Strain and place in caramelized mold. Place mold in a pan of simmering water in the bottom half of the oven.

Cook for approximately 45 minutes or until a knife inserted in the mold comes up dry.

Turn onto platter. If any caramel remains in bottom of the mold, set over low heat until it is loosened and pour over custard.

*1¼ cups sugar*
*2 tablespoons water*
*1 ripe banana, sliced*
*¼ cup raisins*
*5 large eggs*
*5 egg yolks*
*¾ cup milk*

■ *Bonus Recipe*

## SPINACH ROLLS IN PASTRY

Preheat oven to 350 F. Cut one sheet of philo dough into three strips lengthwise. Reserve extra dough under a slightly dampened cheesecloth.

Brush strips with melted butter and fold into thirds lengthwise.

Place one teaspoon of mixture at the bottom of the strip and fold over and over in the form of a triangle as you would a flag. When folded, brush with more butter.

When all the mixture is used up, bake on a buttered baking sheet for 20 minutes or until golden brown.

The spinach rolls can also be placed on a tray, frozen, and then stored loosely in a plastic bag.
Yield: 4 dozen.

*½ pound philo or strudel dough leaves*
*½ cup unsalted butter, melted*
*2 cups spinach mixture (see page 72)*

## MARCELLA HAZAN

# The Italian Way to a Better Meal on a Tighter Budget

**MENU**

Rice and Peas Soup
Braised Pork Chops with Tomatoes and Sage
Fried Broccoli Florets
Macerated Orange and Banana Slices

Total Cost of Dinner for 6: $12.00–$14.00

Bonus Recipe: Broccoli Salad

Wine: California Chablis
*(Cost not included)*

Marcella Hazan *has been described as America's premier teacher of northern Italian cooking. She is the author of* The Classic Italian Cook Book, *and her recipes have appeared in numerous magazines and newspapers throughout the United States. In 1967, she and her husband, Victor Hazan, an Italian-born American, came to New York where she began teaching Italian cooking in her home, translating Italian ingredients and techniques for the American kitchen.*

ll good meals, whether they are improvised or formal, fancy or plain, must ultimately share one paramount objective: to satisfy. In America we are accustomed to meals that revolve about a massive main course and rely for satisfaction upon large portions of what is usually the most elaborate, time-consuming and expensive dish to prepare. Of course it can be satisfying to dig into big helpings of something good, but it is a spendthrift and even monotonous approach to meal planning.

Italians, who have had several centuries in which to learn how to eat well on very little money, have another way. They divide up the meal into a variety of small courses of equal importance and interest wherein each ingredient has been given the opportunity to express fully its flavor and character. This is not a "star" system where shadowy supporting roles are assigned to foods or dishes that may be modest in cost or appearance yet are immensely satisfying. A rice dish or a vegetable gets equal billing with the meat. In this an Italian meal follows the natural inclinations of our palate which responds not to status but to taste. A magnificent soup in which real vegetables, good broth, some beans and a ham bone have slowly released and fused their flavors can give as much joy to the guest (and luster to the cook) as the most prepossessing roast.

In good cooking, as distinguished from show-off, fancy cooking, flavor is what matters most. The good cook is one who shops carefully for honest materials and husbands their natural flavors and textures lest they be wasted or lost on the way from the kitchen to the table. Extracting from good ingredients all the taste and satisfaction of which they are capable is what cooking and economy are all about. Economy in cooking does not mean that you must learn to eat a little less well. What it really means is that you must learn to be a little better cook.

Here are some of the sensible ways of the good cook that are as effective in saving money as they are in saving flavor:

■ Use commercially processed, packaged foods as rarely as possible. All you are paying for is fancy packaging, slick advertising and costly distribution. Learn to make your own mayonnaise. It will add glory to an infinite range of simple, cold dishes. Avoid bottled salad dressings like the plague. They are expensive junk. Oil, vinegar and salt, freshly mixed at home, is all you need to season the most splendid salads. Instead of stocking your cupboard with canned bouillon, stock your freezer with meat scraps and bones. They will make a marvelous light stock that will improve the flavor of every dish where it is used.

■ Concentrate on freshness. Use vegetables in season when they are naturally ripened and full of flavor. Shop for quality, not for bargains. Good produce is always a better value because it has more flavor and less waste. Do not buy such things as grated cheese. It is worthless. Grate your own cheese as you need it from a piece that you keep tightly wrapped in foil in the refrigerator. Do not stock up on bottled herbs and spices. Buy no more than you need for brief periods and buy fresh herbs when available. Even better, grow your own on your windowsill. Do not buy ready ground pepper. Grind your own.

■ Do not rely exclusively on food processing appliances. Their assistance can sometimes be indispensable, but often what you save in time you waste in flavor and texture. Machines tend to flatten, homogenize, weaken the character of the food they process. Moreover, if you are not feeding a crowd, chopping and beating by hand does not take substantially more time than cleaning, washing, and reassembling the machine that has done the work for you.

The menu that follows is composed in the traditional Italian style and, demonstrates how honest, good cooking can make out of economical materials a meal that is elegant, varied, nutritious and, most of all, satisfying.

### RICE AND PEAS SOUP
#### Risi e Bisi

*1½ pounds fresh peas, in their pods*
*2 tablespoons vegetable oil*
*3 tablespoons butter*
*3 tablespoons chopped onion*

This lovely, dense rice and pea soup comes from Venice, a city whose cooking is at the same time frugal and delicate. The ideal peas to use are those very sweet, young, freshly picked peas that, unfortunately, rarely appear in our city markets. However, there is an ingenious way Italians have with mature peas that makes them taste much younger than they are. The sweetest part of the pea is its pod and when a quantity of pods, properly trimmed and peeled, is cooked along with the peas, the overall flavor is a pretty good substitute for that of very early peas. This, of course, is an excellent method for making a small quantity of peas go a long way.

Shell the peas and set aside. Keep all the healthy-looking, crisp, unspotted pods and discard the rest. The inside of the pod is lined with a thin, filmlike skin that must be removed to prepare the pods for cooking. Hold a half pod in one hand with the inside facing you, snap the upper end with the other hand and pull down, stripping away the inside skin. If you don't manage to get the entire skin, don't fuss too much. Set aside the skinless portion of the pod, cutting away and discarding the rest. With a little bit of practice you will soon be able to strip clean the entire pod with one smooth, easy motion. Wash all the peas and trimmed pods in cold water, drain, and set aside.

Put the oil, butter, and chopped onion in a soup pot or casserole and sauté over medium heat until the onion is golden.

Add the peas, pods and salt. Stir for a minute or so, then add half the broth. Cover and cook over medium heat for 15 minutes.

Add the rice and the rest of the broth, cover and cook over medium heat for another 16 to 18 minutes or until the rice is done. The rice should be tender but firm to the bite so test it from time to time to make sure it does not overcook. Do not worry if the pods become partly dissolved—it is to be expected. If, when the rice is done, the consistency of the soup is too thin, uncover and boil away some of the liquid.

Taste and correct for salt, allowing for the saltiness of the cheese. Turn off the heat, mix in the grated cheese, then the chopped parsley. Serve immediately.

*¼ teaspoon salt*
*5 cups broth, either home-made or made by dissolving 2 bouillon cubes in 5 cups water*
*1½ cups rice*
*⅔ cup freshly grated Parmesan cheese*
*3 tablespoons chopped parsley*

## BRAISED PORK CHOPS WITH TOMATOES AND SAGE
### Costolette di Maiale in Umido

These tender and juicy pork chops are from Emilia-Romagna, a region celebrated for the quality and variety of its pork products. Mortadella, zampone, cotechino and Parma ham are some of its specialties

*2 tablespoons butter*
*2 tablespoons vegetable oil*
*6 end-loin pork chops*
*⅓ cup of flour spread on a*

*dish or on waxed paper*
*8–10 whole sage leaves*
*½ teaspoon salt*
*Freshly ground black*
*pepper*
*1 cup chopped, canned,*
*peeled tomatoes with their*
*juice*

whose excellence has never been equalled in other parts of Italy—or elsewhere for that matter. In a place where the pig is so thoroughly exploited it was necessary to find many different ways of cooking pork lest people became weary of its taste. Pork chops cooked in this manner are very appealing indeed; they are succulent and savory and acquire a flavor somewhat similar to that of a very tasty chicken.

Choose a skillet just large enough to contain all the chops later without overlapping. Put in all the butter and oil, turning the heat up to medium high.

When the butter foam begins to subside, dredge the chops on both sides in the flour, shake off excess flour and put them in the skillet. Add the sage leaves.

Brown the chops well on each side for about 2 minutes.

Add the salt, pepper and chopped tomatoes with their juice. Cover the skillet, turn the heat down to medium low and cook for about an hour or until very tender.

### FRIED BROCCOLI FLORETS
#### Fiori di Broccoli Fritti

*1 large bunch fresh broccoli*
*2 tablespoons salt*
*1 extra large egg or 2*
*medium eggs*
*1 cup unflavored bread*
*crumbs spread on a dish or*
*on waxed paper*
*⅔ cup vegetable oil*
*Salt*

Carefully detach the florets from the broccoli stalks. (Do not discard the stalks—see Bonus Recipe, page 82.) Wash under cold, running water and set aside.

Add the salt to 2 quarts of water and bring to a broil.

When the water is at a rapid boil, drop in the florets. As soon as the water returns to a boil remove the broccoli with a slotted spoon or colander. Be gentle or they may crumble. Set aside to cool.

When cool, cut the florets lengthwise into pieces no more than 1 inch thick. If some turn out to be a little thinner, it's perfectly all right.

Break open the egg or eggs into a bowl and beat lightly.

Take one piece of broccoli at a time, dip it on all sides into the beaten egg, shake off the excess, then turn it in the bread crumbs, pressing lightly with your fingertips to make sure the bread crumbs stick to the broccoli. Lay the broccoli on a platter until every piece has been dipped and coated.

Put all the oil in a medium-sized skillet and heat up over medium high heat until it is quite hot.

Put in as many pieces of broccoli as will fit loosely in a single layer. When they have formed a crust on one side, turn them. When they have a nice crust on all sides, transfer to a platter on which you have put some paper towels. Sprinkle with salt. Continue in the same manner until all broccoli pieces are done. Serve hot.

## MACERATED ORANGE AND BANANA SLICES
### Arance E Banane Marinate

It is exceedingly rare for an Italian meal at home to end with dessert. People do eat sweets on occasion, but this is usually a part of those delightful ambulatory moments of Italian life that one spends with friends at a cafe at any time from the middle of the morning to the middle of the night. At home, however, even an elaborate dinner will close with a bowl of fresh fruit and nothing else. Occasionally, as a change of pace, fruit is cut in advance and steeped for several hours in juice and sugar. If desired, a liqueur such as maraschino can be added. Here, in this attractive combination of sliced oranges and bananas, is a simple, inexpensive version of a most refreshing and healthful way to end a meal.

*4 oranges*
*2 bananas*
*1 lemon*
*3 tablespoons of granulated sugar (or more, to taste)*
*Juice of 2 oranges*

Peel the oranges, removing all the white pulpy layer under the peel. Cut them into thin slices and discard all the seeds. Put the slices in a bowl.

Peel the bananas. Cut them into disks ¼-inch thick and add them to the bowl.

Grate the entire yellow part of the lemon peel into the bowl. Use a light touch as you rub the lemon against the grater so that you do not dig into the white pulp under the peel.

Add the sugar and the orange juice to the bowl.

Squeeze the juice from *half* the lemon and add it to the bowl.

Mix all the ingredients thoroughly, but gently. Let steep in the refrigerator for at least 4 hours before serving, or overnight.

■ *Note: Any left over can be used the following day served over a scoop of vanilla ice cream.*

■ *Bonus Recipe*

**BROCCOLI SALAD**

The broccoli stalks set aside from the Fried Broccoli Florets (recipe page 80) are excellent in a salad, served either raw or cooked. If raw, they may be served alone or mixed with other greens.

Cut off the tough butts of the stalks and peel away all the dark green skin. Wash thoroughly in cold water, drain and cut into julienne strips about ¼-inch thick. Season with olive oil, vinegar, salt and pepper.

When using the stalks cooked do not cut into strips but, after peeling, cook in boiling water for about 7 to 8 minutes. They should be tender, but crunchy. Cooked stalks may be served warm, seasoned with olive oil and salt alone, or cold, seasoned as above.

# MADHUR JAFFREY

# An Exotic Indian Meal

**MENU**

Chicken in Red Sauce
Rice with Eggplant and Peas
Cucumber Salad
Fruit

Total Cost of Dinner for 6: $14.00

Madhur Jaffrey *is an Indian actress who won the Berlin Film Festival award as best actress in "Shakespeare Wallah." She has written articles for* The New York Times, Holiday, Gourmet *and other publications, and her cookbook,* An Invitation to Indian Cooking, *was published in 1973 by Alfred A. Knopf. Ms. Jeffrey teaches courses in Indian cooking at the James A. Beard School.*

**DINING IN INDIA**

ndians generally do not serve appetizers as a separate course, the way it is customary to in Europe and America. It is quite normal to see a table laden with meats, poultry, fish, relishes, salads, vegetables, bread and rice, all at the same time. The diner then has the option of eating *what* he wants, *when* he wants and in any combination that his fancy seems inclined to at that particular moment.

I have chosen a limited but exciting meal for this book, which consists of chicken in a thick sauce of onions, garlic, ginger, tomatoes, as well as cinnamon, cardamon, cloves and peppercorns; there is an aromatic baked rice which has eggplant and peas in it; and there is a simple salad of cucumber and yogurt flavored with freshly roasted cumin seeds and minced Chinese parsley. Since Indians generally eat "sweets" at tea time, I have left out the dessert altogether. Indians round off their meal with fruit and you can do the same. For this menu, try oranges, peeled and cut into round or melon slices.

**PREPARATION AND TIMING**

The best way of preparing this Indian meal in the shortest amount of time would be to start by cutting up the eggplant, sprinkling with salt and setting aside. Then wash and soak the rice and set that aside too. Now start your chicken. Get it to the point where you can leave the dark meat simmering for 20 minutes. (Use timers, if necessary.) Next, light your oven and continue with the rice recipe, i.e., heat the oil, put in the cumin seeds, fry the onions, sauté the eggplant pieces and sauté the rice. Add the hot water to the rice and keep cooking. If your chicken timer goes off, pause for a second, put the white meat into the pot and reset the chicken timer for 10 to 15 minutes. Go back to your rice and get it into the oven.

Now you can finish off the chicken and get the cucumber salad into the refrigerator. You can also cut up your fruit if you want to prepare it in advance. Remember that once the rice is cooked it will stay warm, if left covered, for about 20 to 30 minutes.

## CHICKEN IN RED SAUCE *

*4½ pounds frying chicken parts ***
*4 tablespoons vegetable oil*
*4 tablespoons sweet butter*
*1½–inch piece of stick cinnamon*
*5 cardamom pods*
*2 bay leaves*
*1 teaspoon whole cloves*
*1 teaspoon black pepper- corns*
*1–2 hot, dried red peppers (optional)*
*3 medium-sized onions, peeled and minced*
*A piece of fresh ginger, about an inch cube, peeled and grated*
*8 garlic cloves, peeled and minced*
*1 16-ounce can whole tomatoes*
*1½ teaspoons salt (or to taste)*
*¼ teaspoon sugar*

*\* Use legs, thighs and breasts or, if you prefer, get 1½ three-pound chickens and cut them up yourself. Separate legs into drum- sticks and thighs and quarter the breasts.*

Remove the skin from all the chicken pieces. Separate the dark and light meat and keep both aside.

Heat the oil and butter in a wide, heavy-bottomed pot or a deep, heavy skillet over a medium-high flame. When hot, put in the cinnamon, cardamom, bay leaves, cloves and peppercorns. As soon as the cloves begin to swell (this should take just a few seconds), put in the red peppers. Stir the peppers around for a second or two.

Now put in the minced onions and fry them on med- ium heat, stirring frequently, until the onions are lightly browned at the edges.

Put in the ginger and the garlic and fry, stirring for a minute. Turn off the heat under the pot.

Take the whole tomatoes out of the can, leaving the liquid behind, and chop them finely. Put the chopped tomatoes and the liquid from the can into the pot with the fried spices and onions. Then put in the salt, sugar and the dark chicken meat. Turn the heat on under the pot and bring its contents to a boil. Cover, lower heat and simmer gently for 20 minutes, stirring every now and then.

Lift off the cover and put in the white meat. Bring to a boil, cover, lower heat and simmer another 10 to 15 minutes or until both light and dark meats are tender.

Using a slotted spoon, lift out all the chicken pieces and place in a bowl. Turn up the flame under the pot to medium and cook, uncovered, stirring all the time, until you have ¾ to 1 inch of thick, dark reddish- brown sauce at the bottom of the pot. Do not let it burn. Adjust heat if necessary.

Put the chicken pieces back in the sauce and roll them around gently. Turn the heat to low to avoid scorching. Once the chicken is heated through and covered with sauce, it is ready to be served.

■ *Note: When eating this chicken, diners should be warned to pick out the whole spices like fish bones and leave them on the sides of their plates.*

\* See Preparation and Timing, page 85.

## RICE WITH EGGPLANT AND PEAS *

Without skinning the eggplant, dice it into ⅓-inch cubes. Put the cubes into a bowl. Sprinkle with ½ teaspoon salt and mix the salt in with your hands. Leave aside for ½ hour.

Wash the rice several times in water. Drain and put in a bowl. Pour 4 cups of water over the rice and leave to soak for ½ hour.

Preheat oven to 325 F.

Heat the oil over a medium flame in a wide, heavy casserole pot. When smoking hot, put in the cumin seeds. Stir. After a couple of seconds, put in the minced onion and fry, stirring until the onions turn brown at the edges.

Squeeze as much water as possible from the eggplant pieces and add them to the pot. Also put in the ginger, garlic, green chili and turmeric. Sauté on medium-low heat for about 5 minutes.

Now drain the rice and add it to the pot. Also add the ground coriander, cumin, 1¼ teaspoons salt and the shelled peas. Keep sautéing for 6 to 7 minutes.

Add ¾ cup hot water and bring to a boil. Cook on a medium flame for about 5 minutes or until the water is almost all absorbed but the rice still looks very wet. Cover the pot tightly with aluminum foil first and then with its own lid. Place in oven and bake 20 to 25 minutes. Lift cover and check to see if rice is cooked. If not, fluff with a fork and leave in oven another 5 minutes.

*1 medium-sized eggplant (about ½ pound)*
*½ teaspoon plus 1¼ teaspoons salt*
*2 cups long-grain rice*
*6 tablespoons vegetable oil*
*¼ teaspoon whole cumin seeds*
*½ cup minced onion*
*½-inch cube of fresh ginger, peeled and minced*
*5 cloves garlic, peeled and minced*
*1 fresh, hot green chili, minced (optional)*
*¼ teaspoon ground turmeric*
*1 teaspoon ground coriander*
*½ teaspoon ground cumin*
*1 cup shelled peas (fresh or frozen; if frozen, thawed)*

## CUCUMBER SALAD *

Place the cumin seeds in a small iron skillet. Roast the seeds on a medium flame until they turn a few shades darker and give off a delicious, nutty aroma.

Put the seeds in a small mortar and crush to a powder.

Put the yogurt in a non-metallic serving bowl and whip it lightly with a fork. Put in the roasted cumin powder as well as all the other remaining ingredients. Mix well, cover and refrigerate.

*½ teaspoon whole cumin seeds*
*1 container plain yogurt*
*1 cucumber, peeled and sliced into thin rounds*
*¾ teaspoon salt*
*3 tablespoons minced Chinese or regular parsley.*

* *See Preparation and Timing, page 85.*

## CARL JEROME

# A Zesty Lamb Menu

**MENU**

Roast Peppers with Anchovies
Braised Shoulder of Lamb with Turnips
Chicory Salad with Mustard Vinaigrette
Apple Grunt

Total Cost of Dinner for 8 to 10: $23.25

Wine: California Cabernet Sauvignon
*(Cost not included)*

Carl Jerome *is Director of the James Beard Cooking Classes. He is a member of the faculty of The Good Cooking School, for whom he recently completed a national lecture-demonstration tour. Mr. Jerome is food consultant to several restaurants, as well as a demonstrator and cookbook author.*

I have chosen a delicious, hearty menu you can feel comfortable serving to both family and guests. We start the meal with roast peppers and anchovies, a colorful and exciting appetite teaser, followed by a subtle marriage of lamb and turnips with an attractive chicory salad. For dessert, there's an old favorite of mine—Apple Grunt.

If you don't want to bother with a first course for just the family, the peppers can be served with the main course, sprinkled with a few drops of lemon juice and some chopped parsley. Or you might try sliced, hard-boiled egg in place of the anchovies. The really budget-minded will roast a few extra peppers, especially if they happen to be on sale as they were the day I bought them, and use them in salads, or perhaps a quiche. Roasting the peppers, while a little time-consuming, is well worth the effort as it gives the peppers a tantalizing new texture and taste.

The braised shoulder of lamb with turnips is an honest and wholesome use of a cut of meat far too often ignored and one which is as much as 40 to 50¢ a pound less than some of the more commonly used cuts of lamb. It has a robust, juicy flavor that makes it an excellent roast. The bones from the roast, which would usually be discarded, are used to make a quick stock. A quart of store-bought stock, which is chemical in taste and much less satisfactory, would cost about six times as much as making your own. Especially if you happen to have an extra carrot, or a few ribs of celery left in the refrigerator. The turnips are wedded to the lamb during the braising, imparting some of their taste to the braising liquid. Braising, which is a way of using some of the less expensive cuts of meat, always requires a stock, so make extra and freeze it.

The chicory salad is served with a mustard-flavored vinaigrette. And remember, a vinaigrette is a very personal thing. I like the strong, fruity taste of the olives to come through with just a hint of vinegar. But feel free to add as much vinegar as you like. If you have some of that coarsely cracked French mustard, those little bits of mustard seed make a beautiful combination of textures with the chicory.

The Apple Grunt is a delicious apple dessert, so much a part of our heritage. And it is one of my favorites because it can be made in 5 or 6 minutes. The whipped cream pastry is so easy to make that you will find yourself wanting to make fruit cobblers of all kinds —I like using plums, cherries and pears when in season, as well as the apples.

I suggest a California Cabernet Sauvignon to accompany the meal. This is one of America's finest varietal wines, with a rich, full taste, and at a moderate price it's a beautiful complement to this meal.

### ROAST PEPPERS WITH ANCHOVIES

*10 sweet red peppers*
*1 2-ounce can anchovy filets*
*in olive oil*
*Olive oil*
*Oregano*

Arrange the peppers on a broiling rack over a roasting pan. Broil, about 1 inch from the heating element, turning the peppers every 6 to 8 minutes until the entire surface is blistered and charred. Remove, and when cool enough to handle easily, peel the skin and discard the stem and seeds. Cut the peppers into julienne strips and arrange on a platter.

Top the peppers with the anchovy filets, sprinkle lightly with olive oil, and dust with finely crumbled oregano. Serve tepid as a first course or, without the anchovies, as a vegetable with the lamb roast.

### BRAISED SHOULDER OF LAMB WITH TURNIPS

*1 shoulder roast of lamb,*
*about 5 pounds*
*4 pounds turnips*
*1 quart Quick Lamb Stock*
*(recipe follows)*
*Salt and pepper to taste*

Have the butcher bone and roll a shoulder roast of lamb. The roast should be from the blade and arm sections, not the neck or foreshank. The fell, or skin, and excess fat should be removed and discarded; the bones cut into 2-inch pieces and reserved for the stock.

Peel the turnips and cut into ⅜-inch thick slices.

Bring the lamb stock to a boil in a braising pot large enough to hold the roast and the turnips. Put the roast into the pot, cover, and place in a preheated 350 F. oven for 40 minutes.

Remove lamb from the oven, scatter the turnips around the roast, and return to the oven for another 20 to 30 minutes, or until the internal temperature of the lamb registers 135 F. on a meat thermometer.

Remove the meat from the pan and allow to set for 10 minutes before slicing. In the meantime strain the braising liquid into a large-bottomed pan.

Leave turnips in braising pot, cover and keep hot by

returning to the oven, now turned off and the door left slightly ajar.

Reduce the braising liquid over high heat, skimming any fat that rises to the surface. Taste, and season with salt and pepper.

Slice the roast and serve with the turnips on warmed plates. Either spoon some of the reduced braising juices over the lamb and turnips, or pass separately.

■ *Note: For the adventurous who feel deft at butchering, there's an additional economy. The shoulder is not difficult to bone and you can save considerably by boning it yourself. First, slide your well-sharpened boning knife under the ribs to separate the meat from the bones. You'll have to work gradually across the shoulder but it's really much easier than it looks. Then carefully work your knife under the connecting piece of neckbone, which is perpendicular to the ribs, and save the bones for your stock. Now you'll have to make a gash in the underside of the shoulder and, keeping your knife as close to the shoulder blade as possible, separate it from the meat. There will be a protrusion in the shoulder blade, but just keep the knife close to the bone and follow the curves. Be careful not to pierce the meat as it will make rolling the roast difficult. When you reach the arm joint, cut down through the cartilage and remove the blade. Then, cut out the top of the arm bone. Make sure all the fell and excess fat have been removed before you roll and tie the roast.*

## QUICK LAMB STOCK

Combine all the ingredients in a large pot and, over high heat, bring to a boil. Reduce heat and simmer, occasionally skimming the fat that rises to the surface, for 40 to 45 minutes. Strain and refrigerate until needed. (This can be made the night before.)

Makes about 1 quart of lamb stock.

*Lamb bones from the boned shoulder roast (about 2 pounds)*
*1 carrot, roughly sliced or a handful of carrot leaves*
*1 celery rib, roughly sliced or a handful of celery leaves*
*4 or 5 sprigs of parsley*
*1 medium onion, roughly sliced*
*1 clove*
*1 bay leaf, cracked into 3 or 4 pieces*
*½ teaspoon peppercorns*
*2 teaspoons thyme*
*2 garlic cloves, unpeeled*
*6 cups cold water*

## CHICORY SALAD WITH MUSTARD VINAIGRETTE

*2 heads of chicory*

Carefully pick over the chicory, wash and dry. Tear the greens into bite-sized pieces and chill, either in a plastic bag or wrapped in a damp linen kitchen towel, until needed. Just before serving, dress the salad with a mustard vinaigrette.

### Mustard Vinaigrette

*½ cup olive oil*
*2 tablespoons vinegar or more or less to taste*
*1 tablespoon Dijon mustard, not the ball park type*
*Salt*
*Pepper*

Combine oil, vinegar, mustard and salt and pepper to taste. Just before serving, toss salad with enough dressing to coat each leaf. The best way to do this is with your hands.

## APPLE GRUNT

*1½ pounds apples, preferably greenings or pippins*
*6 tablespoons butter*
*6 tablespoons pure maple syrup or brown sugar*
*¼ cup sugar*
*1 cup self-rising flour*
*1 cup heavy cream, whipped to soft peaks*

This version of Apple Grunt, which is very much like a cobbler, is brother of the Apple Slump and first cousin of the Blueberry Buckle, all New England desserts popular from the late seventeenth century to the very early twentieth century.

Peel, core, and cut the apples into large chunks. Scatter the apples in a heavily buttered loaf pan. The one I use is $3¼ \times 5¼ \times 2⅔$ inches. Dot with the butter and spoon the maple syrup over the apples. Fold the sugar and self-rising flour into the whipped cream to form a soft dough. Using your fingers, press the dough evenly over the apples. Bake in a 350 F. oven for 55 to 60 minutes.

Cool slightly, run a knife around the sides of the pan and unmold the Grunt by inverting it onto a plate. Serve warm with either pouring cream or additional whipped cream.

# BARBARA POSES KAFKA

# A Meatless Meal

**MENU**

Eggplant Orientale
Chickpeas with Sesame Oil
Cheese Soufflé
Bulgar Wheat
French Bread
Poached Pears with Raspberry Sauce

Total Cost of Dinner for 6: $14.00

Wine: Côtes-du-Rhône *or* Sancerre
(*Cost not included*)
Espresso or Camomile Tea (for the sleepless)

Bonus Recipes: Main Course Kasha, Pear Ice

Barbara Poses Kafka, *a well-known writer on food and wine, is currently associated with* The Good Cooking School. *She has written for* Vogue, Harper's Bazaar, Wine Magazine, Ladies' Home Journal, *as well as writing a weekly column for* Playbill *for many years. Ms. Kafka edited and wrote the recipe notes for* The Art of Cuisine, *containing the recipes and graphics of Toulouse-Lautrec, and was a contributor to* House & Garden's New Cook Book.

ne of the easiest ways to decrease food costs
is to eat less meat. This does not neces-
sarily mean a vegetarian way of life. It may
mean a smaller percentage of meat in the
meal as in stews and cassoulets. This is the way much
of the world eats, getting most of its proteins from
grains. We can learn from other countries how to eat
foods that are a pleasure as well as being nutritionally
sound and inexpensive.

One of the arguments for eating less meat is that the
world cannot afford to produce protein by feeding grain
to animals. Whether you are concerned with this problem or not, it is one that you will hear more about with
the passing years. In any case, the people who are in-
terested in the meatless solution for moral or economic
reasons have done a great deal of research from which
we can all benefit. If you read *Diet for a Small Planet*
by Frances Moore Lappé you may not be convinced by
the author's arguments but you will certainly know how
to create a meal that is nutritionally sound, though
meatless.

The crux of the meatless problem for nutrition is the
correct intake of protein and some of the B vitamins.
These vitamins are obtainable from dairy products and
wheat germ and the protein problem is one that is
solved by balancing the kinds of food eaten in one meal.
There are 22 amino acids (protein components) that
the body needs to do its work. Eight of these cannot be
synthesized (made by the body). Therefore, they must
be eaten. The problem is, they don't work if they are
eaten separately; they must be eaten at the same time
for the body to be able to use them. The easiest way to
get them all together is by eating meat or eggs; but the
trick can be turned with much less expensive ingredients such as the standard rice and bean combinations
of many of the poorest countries of the world.

Once you read a book such as Lappé that tells you
what to do, the hows can be fascinating. The hunt is on
for the cultures that have traditionally eaten in this
way. Read the counter-culture cookbooks such as
*Country Commune Cooking* by Lucy Horton and find
out how to make your own tofu, the elegant soybean
cake so much used in Chinese and Japanese cooking. It
is one of the most complete proteins you can eat and

one of the most inexpensive. Its uses are seemingly endless in vegetable dishes and soups.

Read *A World of Vegetable Cookery* by Alex D. Hawkes for the joy of it and also to learn new approaches. Read Pakistani cookbooks; they haven't eaten meat there for thousands of years. Remember to think about the wonderful vegetable soups which are the basic food of French peasant life and turn to the rich vegetable stews of Provence.

Experiment with spices. They will give a complexity of tastes to replace that lost by abandoning meat. Cumin, chili pepper and coriander are some that you may not have used much but that go extremely well with grains. Learn about all the grains such as couscous and bulgar wheat, and the dried legumes such as chickpeas and soybeans that you may not have used before. Find out that certain vegetables such as mushrooms, eggplants and okra seem to have a density of taste and texture that satisfies the craving for meat.

This menu is extremely well-balanced nutritionally and not at all eccentric! It is elegant enough for almost any occasion and I don't think anyone will miss the meat. The cost for six people is under $14 with dividends to start you well on the way to two more dinners. The taste is rich enough to support the robust, if uncomplicated, Côtes-du-Rhône red wine. On a warm day, however, you might find it more refreshing to try a well-chilled white Sancerre.

I only hope I can encourage you to learn and experiment. That is one of the greatest pleasures of cooking and eating.

### EGGPLANT ORIENTALE

3 large eggplants, altogether about 3 pounds
1 large yellow (not Bermuda) onion
2 sweet green peppers
1 cup vegetable oil
1 pound can whole tomatoes
1 large clove garlic
2 tablespoons tomato purée
2 tablespoons ketchup
2 tablespoons chili sauce

This recipe comes from the Russian Tea Room, a restaurant near Carnegie Hall in New York filled with musicians, writers, dancers and people who love to eat. The lovely, cold and spicy eggplant purée can be served as a first course or, more plentifully, garnished with romaine lettuce, slices of sour dill pickles, cherry tomatoes and hunks of heavy dark pumpernickel bread as a light main course, a late-night supper dish or for lunch in the summer. You need less than half this quantity to make a first course for six, but the dividend keeps well. Try it as a side dish with meatloaf or as a cooling counterpart to curried rice.

*2 tablespoons tomato paste*
*Pinch cayenne pepper (less than ⅛ teaspoon)*
*4 teaspoons Kosher or sea salt*
*5 grinds black pepper*

With a peeler, skin the eggplants; chop them finely. Peel and finely chop the onion. Remove the seeds from the peppers and chop them finely. In a heavy-bottomed 3-quart saucepan—not aluminum—heat ⅓ of the oil over medium heat. Sauté the onions, without browning, stirring with a wooden spoon. When they are translucent, add the green peppers and continue stirring and cooking until the peppers have the same texture as the onions. Add the rest of the oil and the eggplant. Continue cooking over medium to low heat, stirring occasionally, for thirty minutes.

Drain the tomatoes, saving the juice to add to a soup or a stew. Chop the tomatoes; peel, crush and finely mince the garlic. Add them to the saucepan along with the tomato purée, ketchup, chili sauce and tomato paste. Cook, stirring well, for another 10 minutes. Add seasonings. Put in refrigerator to cool. It will cool more quickly in a metal bowl. It should cool for at least two hours although it doesn't have to be very cold.

This recipe can easily be prepared several days ahead as long as it is tightly covered.

## CHICKPEAS WITH SESAME OIL
### Hummus

This is a dish with variants from most of the Near Eastern countries. Traditionally, it is served with olive oil and chopped parsley sprinkled on top. It can be served on the same plate with the eggplant. It can be used as a dip with raw vegetables or it can be served over romaine lettuce as a salad dressing. It keeps very well in a jar in the refrigerator.

*1¼ cups dried chickpeas or one can, drained*
*¼ cup sesame oil*
*¾ cup peanut oil*
*1 large clove garlic, peeled*
*Juice of 2 large ripe lemons*
*Salt to taste*

If using dried chickpeas, which will be less expensive, the night before cover with cold water and leave out to soak. Before preparing, simmer in the same water for an hour and a quarter or until tender; drain, saving the liquid to use in vegetable soup. If using canned chickpeas, drain, saving liquid in the same way.

Place all ingredients in the blender until smoothly puréed. Add salt gradually, tasting. It will need less than you might suppose because of the large quantity of lemon juice. If warm chickpeas have been used, chill Hummus in refrigerator. Serve cool, not cold.

## CHEESE SOUFFLE

*1 teaspoon plus 4 table-
spoons unsalted butter at
room temperature
5-ounce wedge imported or
domestic Parmesan cheese
5 ounces Jarlsberg or im-
ported Swiss cheese
½ cup flour
1 cup milk
Small pinch cayenne pepper
7 eggs, separated*

This soufflé is very easy to make. Put it in the oven just as everybody is sitting down to dinner. It and the people should be ready at the same time! I use a three-quart glass soufflé dish. If you are using porcelain, add seven minutes to the cooking time and start it a little before people sit down. To put a collar around the soufflé dish, cut a 30-inch length of regular-width wax paper. Double it over along its length to make a long, narrow strip. Wrap it tightly around the soufflé dish, allowing half of it to stick up over the rim of the dish. Tape it in place; then tie a string tightly around it one inch down from the top of the dish. The tape won't hold in the oven but it will keep you from a futile struggle with slipping paper while you are trying to tie the knot.

Heat oven to 375 F. Place shelf in center of oven; put on it a heavy baking sheet to help diffuse the heat. With 1 teaspoon of butter, grease the inside of the soufflé dish and the wax paper. Grate the cheeses and mix them together.

In the top of a double boiler, over simmering water, melt 4 tablespoons butter; add the flour, stirring with a rubber spatula, to make a smooth paste; cook for 5 minutes. Slowly add the milk, stirring constantly; if you have any trouble with lumps, remove the top part of the double boiler from the water and beat like crazy with a whisk. Over the hot water cook, stirring constantly, until smooth and thick. Add cayenne pepper. Remove from the water.

While cooling, beat the egg yolks until very thick. Mix yolks and cheese with contents of double boiler. Wash beaters with soap and rinse and dry well; then beat egg whites until they are stiff but not dry. Fold the egg whites into the cheese mixture one-third at a time. Each addition of egg whites can be a little less well mixed in than the one before. Pour mixture into the prepared soufflé dish and place in center of preheated oven. Bake for 40 minutes. Serve immediately.

## BULGAR WHEAT
### Kasha

*2 tablespoons butter
1 large onion, peeled and
chopped*

This is an optional addition to the meal for those of you whose friends have super hearty appetites and would like the equivalent of rice with their soufflé. This recipe is more flavorful than rice and has an interesting texture.*

Melt butter in a saucepan with a tightly fitting lid. Over medium heat sauté the onion, stirring occasionally, until it is yellow; add the celery and the parsley and continue to cook and stir for three minutes. Add the kasha, salt and pepper and cook, stirring, for 5 minutes. Add the water, stir, bring to a boil; reduce to a simmer; cover and cook for 25 minutes.

*2 ribs celery, scrubbed and chopped*
*½ cup parsley leaves, washed and chopped*
*1 cup Bulgar wheat (kasha)*
*2 teaspoons salt*
*2 grinds black pepper*
*2 cups water*

## POACHED PEARS WITH RASPBERRY SAUCE

Wash pears; leave stem on. In a pan just large enough to hold all the pears standing up, bring the water and sugar to a boil. Squeeze in the juice from the lemon and throw in its shells; don't worry about pits. Add the cloves and nutmeg. Reduce heat so water barely bubbles. Add pears. Increase heat if needed so water continues to bubble. The pears will float so it is necessary to turn them from time to time to make sure that they cook evenly. Cook for 20 minutes.

Remove pears from liquid with a slotted spoon (save liquid for Bonus Recipe following). Holding one pear at a time in a dish towel so you won't burn yourself, pull off the skin with the tip of a paring knife. If the skin will not pull off, rub the dull edge of the knife over the skin. This will loosen it so that it will come off easily. Put the pears in a serving dish in the refrigerator, covered, for at least 3 hours or overnight.

Just before serving, put the defrosted berries and the lemon juice in the blender for a minute at high speed. Pour through a sieve onto the pears. Serve with knife and fork and spoon.

**Pears**

*6 Comice or Bartlett pears, half ripe, unblemished*
*10 cups water*
*2½ cups granulated sugar*
*1 lemon*
*2 cloves*
*Sprinkle nutmeg*

**Sauce**

*1 package frozen raspberries, defrosted*
*Juice of 1 lemon*

## ■ *Bonus Recipes*

### MAIN COURSE KASHA

Use the same ingredients as in the optional Kasha recipe (page 100) or double the amounts if you wish to make both that recipe and this. Add ½ teaspoon of ground cumin, a clove of minced garlic and, if you wish, use broth instead of water; stir in a large handful

---

*\* There are many other uses for this nutritious base—see the Bonus Recipe this page.*

of leftover meat cut into ½-inch cubes and—with
salad—you have an entire meal. Or, having cooked the
kasha the same way but with water and no meat, fill a
shallow greased casserole; make hollows in the kasha
with back of a tablespoon; break a raw egg into each
hollow and place in a preheated 400 F. oven for 15
minutes or until the eggs have set—another complete
meal.

### PEAR ICE

After you have finished poaching the pears in the
recipe on page 101, put the peels back into the poaching
liquid. Boil to reduce by one-third. Put through a sieve
and place in a metal bowl in the freezer. Every two
hours, beat with whisk or mixer at high speed and replace in freezer. Eventually you will have a light and
elegant fruit ice to serve another day. If you are keeping the fruit ice for more than one day, place in tightly
closed containers. It looses quality after a week.

## JEANNE LESEM

# A Creole-Style Dinner

**MENU**

Crudités with Remoulade Sauce
Fish Étouffée
Chocolate Pecan Pie

Total Cost of Dinner for 6: $9.42

Jeanne Lesem, *Food Editor of United Press International, learned to cook during the Depression while helping her mother prepare meals in the family's large, old-fashioned kitchen in North Little Rock, Arkansas. Her first book,* The Pleasures of Preserving and Pickling, *will be published in 1975.*

ime and America's appetite have put Creole and Cajun seafood favorites such as shrimp and oysters into the luxury class, but economy is at the heart of the Louisiana kitchen, and many traditional favorites can still be prepared at reasonable cost in both time and money.

In all likelihood, main dishes such as jambalaya and red beans with rice evolved from thrifty cooks' desire to use up leftovers. Into the jambalaya went scraps of ham, chicken (or once-plentiful game), and shellfish from the Gulf of Mexico and the inland rivers and bayous. Mixed and cooked with rice, tomatoes, onions, garlic and other aromatic herbs, they made a richly satisfying meal. The rice and beans also made a balanced meal, flavored and fleshed-out with a leftover hambone.

The "po'boy" is another complete meal in the Creole tradition whose ingredients depend in large degree on the state of one's appetite and finances. This giant sandwich turns up elsewhere as a hero, grinder or submarine. The Louisiana version consists of a generous piece of French bread, sliced lengthwise, and filled with almost anything from cold, boiled potato slices and other inexpensive vegetables to breaded, fried oysters.

My version of étouffée is economical if you base your choice of fish, as Louisiana cooks do, on local supplies —catfish from a nearby lake or river, or saltwater fish caught in your area. The chopped vegetables that smother it are inexpensive, particularly if they come from your own kitchen garden.

Pass a bowl of steaming, boiled rice for guests to add, as desired, to each serving of the fish filets in their broth, and make at least one 8- or 9-inch square pan of cornbread for sopping up the broth. If you want to be sure of seconds of cornbread for everyone, make two pansful (which will add only pennies to your cost). Any leftovers can be split, toasted, and topped with creamed, chipped beef or chicken à la king or home-made chili. Or in southern tradition, crumble the left-over cornbread and make it into poultry stuffing. If you have leftover pecans from the pie, break them coarsely and add to the stuffing, too.

My menu strays from strict tradition by substituting inexpensive raw vegetables for $2- to $3-a-pound shrimp, to go with the Remoulade Sauce, that delectable blend of homemade mayonnaise with herbs and spices. With crudités as an appetizer, and vegetables in the étouffée, there is no need for other vegetables to accompany the main course, or a salad to follow.

My servings of étouffée are modest in protein content, but there is plenty of supplementary protein—all those eggs in the Remoulade Sauce, the cornbread, and the pie.

I am assuming that you buy rice in raw form (not converted or quick-cooking) in 5-pound bags. After all, rice keeps almost indefinitely if you store it in a tightly closed container in a cool, dry place (not the refrigerator).

I am also assuming you will make your own cornbread instead of buying a mix, which is not only costlier, but also too sweet for this meal. One or two tablespoons of sugar is ample for any cornbread recipe— just enough to encourage browning without making the bread taste like cake.

The price of the dinner, incidentally, reflects not just the three basic courses, but also the rice, the cornbread and a beverage such as coffee or tea.

I usually serve the Crudités and Remoulade Sauce with predinner drinks. I do not serve wine with the Fish Etouffée because its somewhat acid tomato-flavored broth would clash. But if your guests enjoy beer, you might offer it instead.

### CRUDITÉS WITH REMOULADE SAUCE
**A variety of raw vegetables**

There are probably as many different recipes for Remoulade Sauce as there are cooks in Louisiana. Remoulade Sauce is traditional there with cold meat, fish and seafood, but it also makes a richly delicious dip for raw vegetables.

About $1.00 worth of fresh, seasonal vegetables should be plenty as an appetizer for 6 persons. Some possibilities are sticks cut from carrots, young turnips, bell peppers, small zucchini squash, cucumbers, and broccoli and cauliflower stems; whole radishes and scallions, cauliflowerets and broccoli florets. And, of course, celery sticks, including any celery left over from the Fish Étouffée recipe which follows.

## For Remoulade Sauce (1½ cups)

Place raw egg yolk and yolk of hard-cooked egg in a 1-quart bowl. With a wooden spoon force white of cooked egg through a coarse strainer into a small container; cover and refrigerate.

To egg yolks add mustard, salt, cayenne pepper and half the vinegar. Beat with an electric hand mixer on high speed about 1 minute, or until smooth.

Add oil in a very thin stream while continuing to beat at high speed. When the mayonnaise starts to thicken, add remaining oil at a faster rate until all of it is incorporated. Stir in remaining vinegar and thin, if desired, with additional vinegar and/or hot water.

Stir in remaining ingredients. Refrigerate, tightly covered, at least 2 hours for flavors to blend.

At serving time, fill a large bowl or deep platter with cracked ice. Sink the salad dressing bowl in it within an inch of the top. Fill dressing bowl with the sauce and garnish with reserved egg white. Place vegetables directly on the ice.

*1 raw egg yolk*
*1 hard-cooked egg*
*1 teaspoon Creole or Dijon-style mustard*
*⅛ teaspoon salt*
*2 pinches cayenne pepper*
*1 tablespoon red or white wine vinegar*
*1 cup mild-flavored salad oil*
*¼ teaspoon crushed garlic*
*2 tablespoons chopped fresh parsley*
*1 tablespoon chopped fresh or frozen chives*
*½ teaspoon dried leaf tarragon*
*1 tablespoon capers, drained and chopped*
*⅛ teaspoon anchovy paste or half an anchovy filet, drained and mashed to a paste (optional)*
*¼ teaspoon bottled horse-radish, or more to taste (optional)*

■ *Note: Chilling the sauce helps preserve its flavor and helps keep any that may be left over safe for future use. (Dishes containing eggs tend to spoil more rapidly at room temperature than eggless ones. Be sure to refrigerate leftover sauce before you sit down to dinner.)*

*Freeze the white from the raw egg to use in a soufflé or meringues or angel cake. If you use them, any leftover anchovy filets can be used to garnish salads.*

*Any leftover vegetables should be refrigerated and used promptly before their flavor and vitamin content are lost. Use in soup or salad. Blender-chopped, they can be stirred into any leftover rice to be reheated in a colander or large strainer set over boiling water.*

*Leftover Remoulade Sauce can be thinned with plain yogurt or buttermilk and makes a creamy salad dressing.*

## FISH ÉTOUFFÉE

Good cooks in Louisiana bayou country use mild, firm, white-fleshed catfish for this spicy stew, the fish filets

*6 scallions, peeled and cut in ¼-inch rounds (use both*

*white and green parts)*
*⅔ cup chopped celery (2
large ribs)*
*¾ cup chopped green
pepper (1 large, about ½
pound)*
*⅓ cup chopped parsley
(large bunch)*
*½ teaspoon chopped garlic*
*1 teaspoon salt*
*1 can (1 pound) tomatoes,
preferably packed in purée*
*2 pounds skinless fish filets
(any lean, firm-fleshed
variety) cut in 2-inch
chunks*
*4 thin slices unpeeled lemon*
*½ teaspoon ground black
pepper*
*¼ teaspoon ground
cayenne, or to taste*
*¾ teaspoon dried leaf
thyme*
*Pinch ground bay leaf or 1
small whole bay leaf*
*3 tablespoons olive oil or
cooking oil*

smothered in chopped vegetables to make a delicious broth. But I find any non-oily, firm-fleshed chowder fish works well: cod, haddock, pollock, cusk, rock cod or grouper, for instance. Fresh fish is, of course, preferable; if you must use frozen filets instead, increase herbs and spices.

Cook the étouffée in a heavy, flameproof casserole that can come to the table. I prefer enameled ironware but ironstone or glass-ceramic will also do.

Mix prepared scallions, celery, green pepper, parsley, garlic and salt in a 1½-pint bowl. Layer this mixture, tomatoes and their purée or juice, fish filets, lemon slices and herbs and spices in a heavy 3½- or 4-quart flameproof casserole with tight-fitting lid. You should have three layers of vegetables and two each of fish, lemon slices and seasonings, the fish filets close together but not overlapping.

Dribble oil over top layer, cover and cook over medium low heat so that étouffée comes slowly to simmer. Simmer only until fish flakes easily when pierced with a fork—about 45 minutes to 1 hour depending on depth of food and type of casserole. Do not stir (which would break the fish), but shake casserole occasionally if necessary to prevent sticking.

Serve in shallow soup bowls with hot, boiled rice as soon as étouffée is done so vegetables remain slightly crisp.

■ *Note: Freeze any leftover broth to add to fish soup or stew and flake leftover fish to make into salad or sandwich filling, bound with either leftover Remoulade Sauce or mayonnaise highly flavored with mustard. Reheating the fish would overcook it—unless you do it quickly in a microwave oven.*

### CHOCOLATE PECAN PIE

*Unbaked pastry shell for 1
single 9-inch pie crust*
*2 squares (1 ounce each)
unsweetened chocolate*
*2 tablespoons butter*
*3 large eggs*
*½ cup sugar*
*1 cup light corn syrup*
*⅛ teaspoon salt*

This recipe is definitely nontraditional but better than plain pecan pie, I think, because the chocolate counteracts excess sweetness.

Preheat oven to 425 F.

In a flameproof 1-cup measure, melt butter and chocolate over lowest possible heat.

Place eggs in a 2-quart bowl and beat lightly with a fork. Add sugar, corn syrup and salt. Beat until well-mixed and thick. Stir in chocolate-butter mixture until smoothly blended. Stir in pecans and vanilla and pour into prepared pastry shell.

Lightly cover fluted edge of pastry with strips of aluminum foil to keep it from browning too fast. Place pie on middle shelf of preheated oven and bake 15 minutes; reduce temperature to 325 F. and bake 25 to 30 minutes more, or until crust is lightly browned and surface of filling is cracked and leaves no indentation when touched lightly with a finger. Remove foil from edge during last 15 minutes of baking time. Filling will rise in oven but settle gradually as it cools.

Cool pie in pan on rack. Serve warm or at room temperature. Don't count on leftovers—even dieters find this pie hard to resist.

*1¼ cups (about 4 ounces) shelled pecans, coarsely broken*
*1 teaspoon vanilla*

## HELEN McCULLY

# How to Make One Small Turkey Go a Very Long Way

**MENU**

Sardines in Pastry with Lemon-Curry Sauce
Scalloped Turkey
Romaine Salad Vinaigrette
Orange Sherbet

Total Cost of Dinner for 12: about $11.95

Wine: California Burgundy
*(Cost not included)*

Helen McCully *is Food Editor of* House Beautiful *magazine. She is the author of many books on food, among them,* Nobody Ever Tells You These Things About Food and Drink, *based on her magazine column, and* Cooking with Helen McCully Beside You. *Her new book,* Waste Not, Want Not, *will be published about September, 1975. Miss McCully is a member of the faculty of The Good Cooking School.*

ou have a choice with my buffet. You can, as I suggest, give a very stylish party for twelve at minimum cost or you can make both casseroles of scalloped turkey and freeze one; make all the sherbet and serve half at two different meals. Thus, two dinners for six for the price of one buffet for twelve. Nice?

Whatever you do, you're going to save money because you are making a small (6 to 8 pounds) turkey go a very long way. Further, you are using only a minimum of so-called expensive ingredients from start to finish—*only* 3 sticks (¾ of a pound) of butter or margarine, *only* ½ cup heavy cream, *only* 4 egg yolks (be sure to freeze the whites and make meringues); *only* 4 oranges (be sure to "candy" the orange rind * and use to garnish cakes, or compotes of fresh fruit, or just as a nice little sweet when your tooth is aching), *only* parsley sprigs (use the stalks in your turkey broth), *only* 3 lemons (here, too, "candy" the rind).

Whatever you do, you will still serve twelve people deliciously from this one cooking spree.

You'll notice that I've "called for" a domestic wine —California Burgundy. I'd like to be specific and suggest you serve Gallo's Hearty Burgundy—an excellent wine that comes in half-gallon jugs (decant it, of course, to serve at the dinner table). As you can see, I belong to the school that likes a sturdy red wine with such sturdy fare as turkey. In fact, I like red wine with chicken, too. Clearly, I don't go along with those who say "white with white, and red with red." Odd? Not really.

## SARDINES IN PASTRY WITH LEMON-CURRY SAUCE

### The Crust

Prepare the crust as directed on package. Divide in half. With the rolling pin encased in a sleeve, roll out on a lightly floured pastry cloth. Roll each half into two 8-inch squares. Cut each square in half. Place two of them on a baking sheet.

### The Filling

Drain the sardines, reserving 2 tablespoons of the oil. Mash the fish with a fork, then mix in the oil, butter, salt, pepper to taste and a few drops of Tabasco sauce.

*1 package (11 or 12 ounces) pie crust mix*
*2 cans (3¾-ounce size) lightly smoked sardines in oil*
*1 tablespoon butter, softened*
*Salt*
*Freshly ground black pepper*
*Tabasco sauce*
*1 egg yolk*

* See recipe for candied orange rind on page 48.

### To Finish the Pastry

Spread half the filling on two of the rectangles, leaving a good quarter inch all around the edges. Dampen the edges with cold water. Cover with the remaining rectangles. Press edges together with your thumb all around. Beat the egg yolk with 1 teaspoon of water. Brush both pastries all over with yolk. The pastry can be made in advance and refrigerated.

### To Bake

Place in a preheated 450 F. oven for 15 to 20 minutes or until puffed and golden. Serve piping hot, cut into strips, with Lemon-Curry Sauce in a sauce boat.

### LEMON-CURRY SAUCE

*2 tablespoons butter*
*½ cup heavy cream*
*Juice of 1 lemon*
*Dash dill seed*
*½ teaspoon curry powder*

Melt the butter. Stir in the cream, lemon juice, dill seed and curry powder. Heat but do not boil.

### SCALLOPED TURKEY

### To Poach the Turkey

*1 6–8-pound turkey,*
*thawed if frozen*
*Giblets from the turkey*
*1 package (6–8-ounce size)*
*commercial stuffing,*
*prepared according to*
*package directions*

Set the giblets aside for the moment. Truss the bird if the market has not already done so and place, breast side down, in a large kettle that has a tight-fitting lid. Add 2 yellow onions, cut in half, skin on, stuck with 2 cloves; 2 carrots, washed, coarsely chopped; 1 large bay leaf; 4 or 5 stalks parsley; 2 celery ribs with leaves, coarsely chopped; 1 tablespoon salt; 6 peppercorns and enough cold water to cover.

Place over medium heat and bring to a boil. Reduce heat, place a piece of waxed paper on top and then the lid and simmer for 1½ hours. At this point, test for doneness. Properly cooked, the breast should be firm, the legs soft and the skin just beginning to shrink from the leg knuckle.

Lift the turkey from the kettle with 2 wooden spoons, draining any liquid from the cavity back into the kettle. Place the kettle with all vegetables back over high heat and reduce to about 4 cups. Strain. Discard the vegetables. Cool the broth.

### The Giblets

Place the gizzard, coarsely chopped, in a small saucepan with enough of the turkey broth to cover it. Bring to a boil, then simmer until almost tender. Add the liver and heart and continue cooking until the gizzard is very tender. Drain the broth back into the kettle. Put the giblets through the finest blade of the meat grinder. Mix into the stuffing. Do not add any liquid.

### The Sauce

Pour the cup of melted butter into a heavy saucepan. Stir in the flour until smooth. Cook over moderate heat, stirring constantly, until mixture froths—about 10 minutes. Do not brown. Add the broth and beat with a wire whip until smooth. Bring to a boil. Add salt, pepper and nutmeg. Season well. Beat the egg yolks and milk together lightly. Stir into the hot sauce, beating briskly. Bring to a boil but do not boil. Finally, stir in the lemon juice and parsley. Seal with plastic wrap and set aside.

### The Turkey

Pull the skin off the bird and discard. Cut off all the meat—every tiny little bit. Discard only bones and gristle. Cut the meat into generous bite-sized pieces.

### To Finish the Scallop

Butter two 1½-quart soufflé dishes or casseroles. Spread half the commercial stuffing mixture over the bottom of each. Spoon about 1½ cups of the sauce over the stuffing. Cover with half the turkey meat and sprinkle with salt and pepper. Add half the remaining sauce to each dish.

Melt 4 tablespoons (½ stick) butter or margarine and mix in the bread crumbs. Scatter half over the sauce in each dish. Bake in a preheated 375 F. oven for 25 minutes or until the scallops are piping hot and golden.

## ROMAINE SALAD VINAIGRETTE

Blend oil and vinegar, salt and pepper. You may adjust vinegar content to suit the salad or individual palate; also salt and pepper to taste.

Wash and dry romaine and place in refrigerator until ready to use. When ready to serve, tear romaine into pieces and toss with dressing.

### Sauce and Topping

*1 cup (2 sticks) butter or margarine, melted*
*1 cup all-purpose flour*
*4 cups turkey broth*
*Salt*
*Freshly ground white pepper*
*Freshly ground nutmeg*
*4 egg yolks*
*1 cup milk*
*Juice of 1 lemon*
*10–15 sprigs parsley, minced (about ½ cup)*
*4 tablespoons (½ stick) butter or margarine*
*1 cup dry bread crumbs*

### The Dressing

*1 head romaine*
*6 tablespoons olive or vegetable oil*
*2 tablespoons wine vinegar*
*½–1 teaspoon salt*
*Freshly ground pepper*

### ORANGE SHERBET

*Grated rind of 3 to 4*
*oranges*
*1 cup orange juice (3 to 4*
*medium oranges), strained*
*Juice of ½ lemon, strained*
*2 cups sugar*
*Few grains salt*
*6 cups milk*

Mix the orange rind, juice, lemon juice, sugar, salt together. Stir in the milk. Continue stirring until sugar has dissolved. At this point it will probably look curdled but don't be alarmed, freezing takes care of that.

Pour into 3 to 4 refrigerator trays. Place in freezer and freeze until the outer edge is solid but center is still mushy. Pour into a large bowl or the bowl of the electric mixer and beat until the sherbet is smooth and fluffy. Pour back into trays and freeze until firm.

To serve, spoon into chilled sherbet glasses. Lacking those, use wine glasses. Chilling is important because sherbet melts quickly once served.

■ *Note: Citrus fruit dropped into boiling water for a few minutes yields more juice. If, however, the recipe calls for the rind, it should be peeled or grated first.*

## GLENNA McGINNIS

# Smoked Tongue Makes Party Fare

**MENU**

Shrimp-Avocado-Orange and Chicory Salad
Boiled Smoked Beef Tongue
Broccoli Superb
Savory Carrots and Onions
Crispy Seeded Bread Rounds
Brownies à la Mode with a Secret *or*
Uncooked Apple Sauce and Sugary Gingersnaps

Cost of Dinner for 6: $11.65

Bonus Recipes: Curried Tongue and Rice Soup
Creamy Meat Hash

Wine: California Burgundy
*(Cost not included)*

Glenna McGinnis *recently retired from* Woman's Day *magazine, where she had been* Food Editor *for over thirty years. A graduate in Home Economics, Mrs. McGinnis has conducted cooking schools throughout the United States, appeared on radio and television, and spoken before numerous groups on her favorite subjects—food, cooking, and home management.* Food Editor *of* The Woman's Day Encyclopedia of Cooking, *she is presently editing, writing, and conducting her own business, Home Economists Unlimited, in Litchfield, Connecticut.*

his colorful dinner is planned for six persons. The portions will be ample and some seconds on main course items are possible.

The first course is a combination appetizer and salad, and the bothersome part of the preparation can be done a day ahead. The readied and chilled ingredients need only be arranged on individual salad plates reasonably close to serving time.

The second course is totally comprised of do-aheads —meat, two vegetables and bread.

For the yummiest of desserts, the preparation is just about *nothing* and may be done early on the day of the dinner.

All this and heaven too, in the thick and meaty soup, a great hash and enough broccoli to serve as a cooked vegetable or raw in a salad for after-the-company-dinner family meals—or any four hungry people. There'll be some leftover brownies, too, if *guarded*.

## SHRIMP-AVOCADO-ORANGE AND CHICORY SALAD
## WITH PIQUANT DRESSING

The day before, boil water, lemon and salt together for 7 minutes. Add frozen shrimp, bring to a boil, reduce heat, cover and simmer for 5 minutes. Remove from heat, uncover, and let cool in water. Drain shrimp, split them lengthwise. Lay them in orderly fashion in covered container in refrigerator.

For fresh shrimp in shells, wash in cold water. Drain and prepare as the frozen shrimp except note how quickly the unfrozen shrimp come to a boil. When cool, remove shells and black veins. *Do not overcook.*

Save and refrigerate or freeze the cooking water to add to homemade soup or other seafood dishes, or to dilute canned soups.

Peel oranges, cutting just through to the flesh. Remove segments and store in plastic bag in refrigerator. (Bags don't have to be washed as containers do at a busy time.) Chill unpeeled avocados, washed and dried chicory and salad plates.

Shortly before serving, line plate with chicory. Peel and halve avocados. Slice avocado halves and prettily arrange with orange segments and shrimp on chicory. Have cut side of shrimp down.

*1 pound shelled, deveined medium-sized frozen, uncooked shrimp or 1¼ pounds fresh shrimp in shell (without heads)*
*4 cups of water*
*2 slices lemon*
*¾ teaspoon salt*
*3 large seedless oranges*
*2 medium or 3 small, ripe but firm avocados*
*Chicory*

Cutting expensive shrimp in half makes it appear you have more. (If budget permits, use more shrimp if desired.) Put shrimp on top where it shows. Immediately cover plates with plastic wrap and return to refrigerator for up to an hour and the avocados will not darken. Serve with Piquant Dressing or pass the dressing, if preferred.

## PIQUANT DRESSING

¾ cup olive oil
1 clove garlic, crushed
⅓ cup white rice wine vinegar
2 tablespoons capers, minced
3 tablespoons chopped pimiento
2 tablespoons chopped chives
1 teaspoon salt
Freshly ground black pepper

Combine all ingredients in shaker. Season with pepper. Refrigerate until 1½ hours before serving.

Shake vigorously and pour over salad or into sauceboat for passing.

1 smoked beef tongue (4 to 5 pounds)
Water
1 tablespoon mixed pickling spices
1 large onion, sliced
1 cup chopped celery tops and leaves
Broccoli leaves for garnish *

* See Broccoli Lore following

## BOILED SMOKED BEEF TONGUE

Although we speak of "boiled" tongue, it actually is slowly simmered, then cooled and skinned. The broth is usable because modern smoked tongues do not make it too salty for use. Cook the tongue 2 or 3 days ahead.

The larger tongue naturally provides more leftovers but a 4-pound one is more common and will adequately serve 6 and leave makings for one or two family dishes. Wash and put tongue into large kettle. Cover with cold water and add spices, onion and celery. Bring to boil, reduce heat, cover and simmer 2½ to 3 hours, or until tender when tested with fork.

Let tongue cool in liquid. Remove and peel skin off. Slit skin carefully across top, not cutting into tongue—sharp scissors are helpful. Wrap in plastic or foil and refrigerate. Strain 2 cups broth into a jar to use for heating sliced tongue for serving. Also strain remaining broth into suitable container and refrigerate or freeze for making Curried Tongue and Rice Soup (see Bonus Recipe page 124) or other soup.

After tongue chills, cut the choice front section diagonally into thin attractive slices. Arrange nicely in a shallow oven proof serving dish. Pour the 2 cups reserved broth over slices. Cover air tight with foil.

Refrigerate until 1½ hours before serving. Heat (covered) in a slow oven 300 F. about 20 minutes. Uncover to serve. Remove almost all of liquid with baster or by pouring it off. (Reserve liquid for soup use.) Sprinkle with minced parsley. Garnish with broccoli leaves. Serve with Dijon mustard on the side.

Be sure to wrap and refrigerate or freeze the remaining back half of tongue for future use.

## BROCCOLI LORE

Buy the handsomest, biggest and greenest bunch of broccoli available. It must be 2½ or more pounds. If in doubt, buy two bunches. Soak in very salty water 1 hour to make sure no worms or bugs are concealed. Rinse. Remove any pretty green leaves and use to garnish tongue dish. They won't wilt from heat as parsley does. Or save, to shred finely and add to cabbage slaw for flavor and color or use in mixed green salad. Cut off the stems about 1 inch below "flower" portion. Reserve upper portion for Broccoli Superb (recipe follows). Save the stem portion and, unless skin is tender, peel with vegetable parer or sharp knife and do any or all of these money stretchers.

Cut thin crosswise slices and serve as scoopers for dips, in green salads, as raw relish or crisp-cook in a little water or by stir-fry method. Use all broccoli or combine with other vegetables—it's lovely with color-contrasting carrots.

Cut stems lengthwise into sticks—thin ones for use as raw relish, fatter ones for crisp-cooking and serving as you would asparagus.

Dice stalks or coarsely shred and crisp-cook or use raw in slaw or tuna and other salads.

## BROCCOLI SUPERB

This *isn't creamed* broccoli. It is gorgeous green broccoli just held together.

*Upper portion large bunch broccoli*
*⅓ cup butter or margarine*
*⅓ cup flour*
*Broccoli cooking liquid*
*Light cream or milk*
*¼ teaspoon freshly grated nutmeg*
*Salt and freshly ground white pepper*
*Paprika*

Finely chop upper portion of broccoli. There should be 8 cups. Cook, covered in a skillet, in very little water until just tender. Drain off liquid into a measuring cup and reserve.

Melt butter or margarine in double boiler. Stir in flour and add cooking liquid plus enough cream or milk to make 2 cups. Whisk until smooth and quite thick.

Add nutmeg, broccoli and salt and pepper to taste. Keep hot over simmering water or, if prepared ahead, cook, cool, and refrigerate and reheat before serving. Mixture may be turned into an ovenproof serving dish. Cover and reheat in oven. Do not overheat or brown. Individual ramekins may be used. Sprinkle with paprika only in center.

## SAVORY CARROTS AND ONIONS

*3 tablespoons butter or margarine*
*6 cups carrots, cut into very thin julienne strips or slices*
*1½ cups chopped onion*
*½ teaspoon crushed dried leaf thyme*
*½ teaspoon crushed dried leaf marjoram*
*½ teaspoon crushed dried leaf sage*
*1 teaspoon salt*
*⅛ teaspoon freshly ground black pepper*

Put all ingredients in top of double boiler. *Add no water.* Stir. Cook, covered, over rapidly boiling water about 35 minutes or until crispy tender. Stir now and then. Add more salt and pepper if needed. If desired, cook ahead and reheat. Do not let water boil dry. Save the scrapings from carrots and cook a bit—then add to dog or cat food—they may like this free dose of vitamins and minerals. Some birds and other pets like raw carrot peelings as well.

## CRISPY SEEDED BREAD ROUNDS

*24 bread slices (any variety but not extra thin)*
*Soft butter or margarine*
*Sesame seed*
*Poppy seed*
*Caraway seed*

Make 24 rounds from bread using the largest round cutter possible. A scalloped-edged one makes slices pretty. An appropriate-sized empty can may be used if a couple of holes are made in the bottom.

Spread bread rounds with butter and place on baking sheet. Sprinkle with choice of seed. Or, do some of each. Cover with plastic film until ready to bake in 325 F. oven until lightly toasted. Rounds may be spread ahead, wrapped and kept a day in cool place, or baked early in day and reheated.

The crusts left from cutting rounds may be used for making crumbs, stuffing, pudding or toasted in the oven and eaten with soups and salads. They may also be used under creamed mixtures.

## EASY BROWNIES

*⅓ cup butter or margarine*
*2 squares (2 ounces) unsweetened chocolate*
*1 cup granulated white sugar*

These are the non-cake-type gooey brownies—hard to beat!

In a heavy saucepan, over low heat, melt butter or margarine and chocolate, stirring constantly. Cool. Beat in sugar and vanilla. Add eggs one at a time and beat well. Add flour, salt, nuts. Mix well.

Pour into greased 8 × 2 × 2-inch or 7 × 9 × 2-inch pan. Bake in center of moderate 350 F. oven for 25 minutes. *Do not overbake.*

Turn out on rack. Cool. Cut 6 3-inch squares for the dessert. Plastic wrap until putting dessert together. There will be some left to cut in smaller pieces for family use. Store air tight. Do *not* bake the brownies in advance of the day of the dinner.

*½ teaspoon pure vanilla extract*
*2 eggs*
*¾ cup sifted flour*
*¼ teaspoon salt*
*¾ cup finely chopped walnuts or pecans*

### BROWNIES À LA MODE WITH A SECRET

Put each brownie in individual bowls or on plates. With sharp knife tip, cut several criss-crossed gashes halfway through top side. When ready to serve, pour one tablespoon liqueur in center of each. Top with ice cream ball or spooned ice cream.

*6 brownies, 3 x 3-inches each*
*6 tablespoons Cointreau (Triple Sec, Grand Marnier, or any orange-flavored liqueurs may be used)*
*1 quart Fudge Swirl ice cream or ice milk*

■*Note: To make serving easier, gash brownies when cutting into squares and place on or in individual serving dish. Plastic wrap. Keep at room temperature. If using ice cream balls, scoop ahead onto foil and store in freezer. Remove while clearing table from main course. If spooning, let ice cream soften a bit at room temperature.*

*Don't forget to have lots of freshly made coffee.*

### UNCOOKED APPLESAUCE

Buzz lemon juice, salt, syrup and sugar in a blender for 30 seconds. Pour into bowl. Core and slice apples into mixture. Cover apples to prevent discoloration. Return to blender and buzz until smooth. Serve at once.

*⅓ cup lemon juice*
*⅛ teaspoon salt*
*⅔ cup light corn syrup*
*2 tablespoons sugar*
*8 red eating apples, chilled*

■ *Note: All except final buzzing may be done a few hours ahead if apple slices are covered in mixture and container is made air tight by covering with plastic wrap. Extrude as much air as possible before wrapping. Refrigerate.*

### SUGARY GINGERSNAPS

Sift dry ingredients together. Cream shortening and sugar. Beat in molasses and egg. Blend in dry ingredients. Make 1-inch balls and roll in sugar. Put 1 inch apart on ungreased baking sheet. Bake in moderate

*2 cups all-purpose flour*
*1 tablespoon ground ginger*
*1 teaspoon ground cinnamon*
*2 teaspoons baking powder*

½ teaspoon salt
¾ cup vegetable shortening
1 cup granulated white
sugar
1 egg
¼ cup dark molasses
Granulated white sugar for
coating

350 F. oven for 12 to 15 minutes. Do not brown. Remove to rack to cool. Store air tight. Makes 5 dozen.

■ *Note: This will give lots of leftover cookies. They keep forever and are so good—and really cheap.*

### LEFTOVER TONGUE TIPS

Cut leftover "back" end of chilled tongue into 1-inch slices. Remove all fat and discard. The lean meat will greatly resemble smoked ham and, when minced, chopped or diced, it may be used as you would ham. Add to baked or other dried bean dishes, macaroni and cheese, scalloped potatoes or egg salad. Cream it and use in spreads, patties, fritters or croquettes. And in potato, bean, lentil or split pea soup. The broth may also be used in the soups.

■ *Bonus Recipes*

### CURRIED TONGUE AND RICE SOUP

2 quarts broth from boiled
smoked tongue
1 cup chopped celery and
leaves
1 cup chopped onion
1 cup chopped carrots
½ cup raw rice (not instant)
2 teaspoons curry powder
2 cups minced, cooked,
smoked beef tongue
Lemon slices
Minced parsley

Skim off any fat on broth. Taste broth. If too salty, dilute with water. Put all ingredients except lemon and parsley in large kettle. Bring to boil, cover and simmer 45 minutes. Serve in large bowls with lemon slice and parsley afloat.

■ *Note: If desired, omit curry powder and add freshly ground black pepper or chili powder to taste.*

### CREAMY MEAT HASH

1 large onion, chopped
2 cups rich milk or light
cream
4 cups raw potato cut in
¼-inch cubes
2 cups chopped, cooked,
smoked beef tongue
1 teaspoon salt
¼ cup minced parsley
Freshly ground black
pepper

This is a superb breakfast, lunch, brunch or supper main dish. It can be made ahead and reheated.

Put onion, milk or cream, potato, tongue and salt in large skillet. Cover and simmer about 20 minutes or until potato is almost tender. Stir in minced parsley. Season with pepper. Cover and simmer until potato is tender. Stir occasionally during cooking.

## PERLA MEYERS

# A One-Dish Peasant Meal

**MENU**

Stuffed Whole Cabbage à la Basquaise
Oranges al Vino

Total Cost of Dinner for 6: $17.30

Bonus Recipes: White Beans à la Catalane
Mediterranean Bean Salad

Wine: California Mountain Red Burgundy
*(Cost not included)*

Perla Meyers *teaches creative cooking in her New York school,* The International Kitchen, *which she founded in 1967. Author of* The Seasonal Kitchen: A Return to Fresh Foods, *Mrs. Meyers' new book,* The Peasant Kitchen, *will be published in 1975.*

ere is a one-dish meal which originated in the Basque country in the southwest part of France. It is in the peasant tradition of European cooking, making the most out of simple and inexpensive ingredients.

This kind of meal, a favorite among French country cooks, does not have a rigid formula, thus allowing you to interpret it to your own taste. It is an all-season dish that uses only what is available at reasonable cost year round in every supermarket. Although the term peasant cooking brings to mind simple, uncomplicated food, it is not without refinement. As a matter of fact, it is a cuisine that is often intricate and sophisticated. The basic idea of peasant cooking is to use regional local produce, be it vegetables, fruit, cheese, meats or wines. Many dishes such as Boeuf Bourgignon and Coq au Vin that are now considered part of *haute cuisine* have originated in the peasant kitchens of France.

In this menu a whole head of cabbage is stuffed with a highly seasoned sausage meat and then braised in a well-flavored broth. The broth is then thickened with cooked white beans and spaghetti, producing a gutsy soup. The stuffed cabbage becomes the main course accompanied by sausages, bacon and a garnish of "all-season vegetables." A loaf of black bread, a bowl of sweet butter and a simple red table wine is all you need to give this meal its finishing touch. A hearty meal like this calls for a light fruity dessert such as the Oranges al Vino.

This kind of cooking stresses simplicity and freshness at all times and, with its direct and economical approach, it is, to my mind, the most suitable for our way of life today.

## STUFFED WHOLE CABBAGE À LA BASQUAISE

### To Make the Stuffing

In a small, heavy skillet heat the butter, add the onion and cook until soft but not browned. Remove and reserve. In a large mixing bowl combine the ground pork, onion, garlic, parsley, salt, pepper, allspice, thyme, egg and breadcrumbs. Work the mixture with your hands until it is well blended. Add 2 tablespoons of water and the optional spinach, taste and correct the seasoning. Set aside.

### The Stuffing

2 tablespoons butter
1 onion, finely minced
1 pound finely ground pork
2 cloves of garlic, mashed
⅓ cup finely minced parsley
Salt
Freshly ground black pepper
Large pinch of allspice
Pinch of thyme

1 egg
½ cup breadcrumbs
1 pound of cooked spinach,
well-drained and chopped
(optional)

**The Cabbage and Soup**

2-pound piece of slab
bacon
1 large cabbage, preferably
Savoy cabbage
3 tablespoons butter
1 cup carrots, finely minced
1 cup celery, finely minced
2 medium onions, peeled
and finely minced
3–4 quarts water or light
beef bouillon
1 large sprig of parsley
1 bay leaf
1 whole head of garlic,
unpeeled
1 dry hot chili pepper
6–8 peppercorns
Salt
6 sausages (optional)

**The Vegetables**

4–6 medium-sized turnips,
peeled and cut in half
4–6 medium-sized all-
purpose potatoes, peeled
and quartered
4–6 young carrots, peeled
and cut in half

**The Soup Garnishes**

3 cups cooked white beans
(see recipe below)
½ cup very thin spaghetti,
broken into 1-inch pieces
Finely sliced French bread
toasted in the oven until
crisp
½ cup coarsely grated fresh
Parmesan

3–4 cups dry white beans
6 peppercorns

**The cabbage and soup**

In a large saucepan bring water to boil, add the bacon and cook for 5 minutes. Drain and reserve.

In a large casserole bring salted water to boil, add the cabbage, head down, and poach it for 5 minutes. Drain the cabbage and dry it with kitchen towels.

Carefully separate the cabbage leaf by leaf. Place a spoonful of the stuffing on each one starting from the middle working outward. Reshape the cabbage with your hands and tie it up with kitchen string so that it will retain its shape during cooking. Set aside.

In a large heavy casserole, heat the butter, add the carrot, celery and onion and cook until soft but not browned. Add the water or bouillon, bacon, parsley, bay leaf, garlic, chili pepper, peppercorns and cabbage. Season with salt. Bring to a boil, reduce the heat and simmer the cabbage tightly covered for 1½ hours.

Add the turnips, potatoes and carrots to the casserole and continue cooking for 20 to 30 minutes or until the vegetables are almost tender. Add the sausages and heat through.

With two large perforated spoons, transfer the cabbage to a serving platter. Add the vegetables, sausages and bacon. (Cut the bacon into serving pieces.) Spoon a little of the broth over the cabbage. Cover the platter and keep warm.

Add the cooked white beans and spaghetti to the broth. Cook for 10 minutes or until the spaghetti is tender. Taste the soup and correct the seasoning.

Place a slice of French bread into each soup bowl, sprinkle with Parmesan cheese and spoon the hot broth over it. Serve immediately.

Follow the soup with stuffed cabbage and vegetables accompanied by black bread and a bowl of sweet butter.

■ *Variation: For a simpler version of this dish you can omit the beans and spaghetti, and serve the clear broth as an appetizer to be followed by the cabbage. If you do not want to include all the vegetables, simply cooked new potatoes will do very nicely too.*

**WHITE BEANS**

Dry white beans are an important staple in European peasant cooking. They are marvelously versatile and go well in many salads, soups and casseroles. When cooking beans I always make an extra amount to be used in the Mediterranean salad (recipe page 130) or as an accompaniment to leftover lamb, hamburgers or pork sausages.

Preheat oven to 300 F.

In a large casserole combine the beans with water to cover, bring the beans to a boil on top of the stove and cook for one minute. Remove the casserole from the heat and set aside for one hour. Add the remaining ingredients and season with salt. Cover the casserole tightly and set in the center part of the oven. Cook the beans for 2 to 3 hours or until tender. Remove the beans from the oven, discard the onions, parsley and herbs. Let the beans cool in their cooking water.

The cooked beans will keep for 2 or 3 days refrigerated.

*1 large sprig of sage* or *1 teaspoon dry sage*
*1 large sprig of thyme* or *½ teaspoon dry thyme wrapped in cheesecloth*
*2 medium onions, peeled and stuck with a clove*
*2–3 unpeeled garlic cloves*
*1 large sprig of parsley*
*Salt*

## ORANGES AL VINO

With a vegetable peeler remove the peel of 2 oranges, being careful not to include the white membrane. Cut the orange peel into fine julienne strips and reserve.

In a small saucepan bring water to a boil, add the orange peel, cook for 5 minutes, drain and reserve.

In a heavy enameled saucepan combine the wine, one cup of sugar, cinnamon stick, cloves and lemon peel. Bring the mixture to a boil, reduce the heat and cook over medium heat until the wine is reduced by ⅓. Whisk in the currant jelly and simmer until the jelly is dissolved. Taste and if the wine seems too sweet, add the lemon juice. Cool the wine mixture.

Peel the oranges with a sharp knife, removing all the white membrane, cut the oranges crosswise into fine slices. Arrange the orange slices in a large glass bowl, sprinkle with the remaining sugar and orange liqueur. Pour the wine over the oranges, garnish with dates and orange peel. Chill for 4 to 6 hours before serving. 30 minutes before serving bring the oranges back to room temperature.

*4–6 navel oranges*
*2½ cups red wine*
*1 cup sugar plus 2 tablespoons*
*1 cinnamon stick*
*2 cloves*
*1 small piece lemon peel*
*½ cup currant jelly*
*1 teaspoon lemon juice*
*3 tablespoons orange-flavored liqueur—Curacao, Grand Marnier or Cointreau (optional)*
*½ cup diced dates for garnish*

■ *Variation: For the dates substitute large prunes that have been cooked until tender in the poaching wine.*

## ■ *Bonus Recipes*

### WHITE BEANS À LA CATALANE

2 tablespoons olive oil
½ cup bacon cut into 1-
inch cubes
2 large onions finely sliced
1 teaspoon finely minced
garlic
2 tablespoons finely minced
parsley
3–4 large tomatoes, peeled,
seeded and chopped
Salt
Freshly ground black
pepper
½ teaspoon dry thyme
1 large sprig of fresh rosemary or ½ teaspoon dry
4 cups cooked white beans
6–8 pork sausages sautéed
in 3 tablespoons olive oil
(optional)

In a large cast iron skillet heat the olive oil, add the bacon and cook until almost crisp. Remove the bacon with a slotted spoon to a side dish and reserve. Discard all but two tablespoons of fat from the pan. Add the onions, garlic and parsley; cook until the onions are soft and lightly browned. Add the tomatoes, salt, pepper, thyme and rosemary. Cook the mixture until all the tomato water has evaporated and the mixture is thick. Add the beans and heat through. Taste and correct the seasoning. Return the bacon to the pan and toss the mixture lightly. Pour the beans into a hot serving dish. Top with sautéed sausages and serve hot with crusty bread.

### MEDITERRANEAN BEAN SALAD

4 cups cooked white beans
(at room temperature)
1 small red onion, finely
sliced
¾ cup finely diced
pimientos
2 tablespoons well-drained
capers
2 tablespoons finely minced
parsley
1 cup flaked tuna
½ cup finely diced green
pepper
Juice of 1 large lemon
6–8 tablespoons fruity
olive oil
Salt
Freshly ground black
pepper
Finely sliced pepperoni
sausage or other spicy
sausage (optional)

In a large serving bowl combine the beans, onion, pimientos, capers, parsley, tuna and green pepper. Set aside. In a small mixing bowl combine the lemon juice, olive oil, salt and pepper. Pour the dressing over the salad and toss it lightly. Taste and correct the seasoning. Garnish the salad with the optional sausage and serve at room temperature accompanied by black bread and sweet butter.

## MAURICE MOORE-BETTY

# An Anglo-Indian Treat

### MENU

Indian River Tomato Consommé
Curried Vegetables
Compote of Pears with Sauce Dijonnaise

Total Cost of Dinner for 6 to 8: $8.50

Beverage: Cold Danish Lager Beer
(*Cost not included*)

Maurice Moore-Betty, *cookbook author, owner-operator of The Civilized Art cooking school, food consultant, restauranteur, is a former British army officer and plantation owner. His books include* Cooking for Occasions, The Maurice Moore-Betty Cooking School Book of Fine Cooking, *and* The Civilized Art of Salad Making.

o appreciate food as well as the arts, a certain amount of exposure to one or the other is necessary. Curry dishes in this country have rarely been popular purely and simply because there has been little or no introduction to this unique flavor, or rather flavors. On the other hand the English during their Indian Empire days, were well-accustomed to curries probably because when they first took up residence in that country it was easier to allow one's cook to prepare what he knew best rather than take the pains to teach him Victorian dishes. A taste developed and soon the benefits of curries in a warm climate were appreciated. Like hot tea on a warm summer's day, the spices caused one to perspire and consequently produced a cooling effect.

I will not involve the reader in the art of blending the spices necessary for each type of fish, vegetable and meat curry, for indeed each one requires separate handling in much the same way that the Westerner varies the herbs and spices needed for poultry, game, fish and meats.

A dish of curried vegetables has been chosen as the mainstay of this menu and I have taken a short route to the finished article by using a commercial blend of spices imported from India erroneously titled "Curry Powder." This I know will cause the specialist in Indian cookery to throw up his hands in horror, but it will suffice to introduce the reader to the flavor and, should it please him, he will no doubt go on from there to learn the art of spice-blending for his own needs.

Choosing vegetables as the main ingredient has the advantage of making the vegetarian happy and pleasing the housekeeper by encouraging her to pull the purse string a little tighter. Rice is the logical accompaniment and one may serve as many side dishes as one likes. I would suggest a few plumped-up raisins, a little shredded coconut and most definitely a Mango Chutney of a recognized brand name.

Wine is rarely drunk with curry because the spices distort the palate, but ice cold Lager beer is ideal, the Danish type in particular. The flavors, color and textures of this menu are, in my opinion, as close to perfection as one can get. The soup is refreshing, the curry stimulating and the poached pears will cool the palate of those non-curry addicts.

Should all of the curry not be used and any soup left over, a splendid soup may be concocted with the use of a blender and additional chicken stock contrived from bouillon cubes or powder.

Curries are usually served in the middle of the day, the thought being that spiced dishes are an inducement to disturbed sleep.

### INDIAN RIVER TOMATO CONSOMMÉ

*1 1-pound can Italian plum tomatoes with basil*
*1 carrot, shredded*
*½ medium onion, chopped*
*1 bay leaf*
*Rind of 1 lemon, grated*
*6 peppercorns*
*3 cups clear chicken consommé*
*2 tablespoons sugar*
*½ cup dry white Vermouth*
*Salt and freshly ground pepper (preferably white)*
*Rind of 1 orange*
*Juice of 1 orange*
*2 tablespoons finely chopped parsley*

In a heavy 2-quart pan bring to a boil, then simmer very gently for 8 minutes, the tomatoes, the carrot, the onion, bay leaf, lemon rind and peppercorns.

Strain carefully into a mixing bowl. Rinse the pot and return the tomato liquid to the clean pot, then add the chicken consommé. Put over moderate heat and add the sugar and Vermouth. Continue heating almost to the boiling point, then season with salt and freshly ground pepper. Proceed carefully as the soup can suddenly become very hot.

Meanwhile, peel the orange very carefully, avoiding the white pith. Cut the peel into very thin strips half an inch long. Put the peel aside to be used as a garnish. Squeeze the orange, adding the juice to the soup and reheat very gently.

Ladle the soup into bowls or soup plates and sprinkle with finely chopped parsley and the orange rind.

This soup may be served hot or cold.

■ *Note: This soup is delicious served cold. It is a refreshing pick-me-up in the morning and makes a superb Bloody Mary mix.*

### CURRIED VEGETABLES

**Curry Sauce**

*2 tablespoons oil*
*2 tablespoons chopped onion*
*2 tablespoons curry powder*
*1 tablespoon flour*
*1 small garlic clove, crushed*
*2 dried apricots, chopped fine*

Heat the oil in a heavy saucepan. Add the onion and cook, stirring for several minutes, but do not burn. Stir in the curry powder and flour and cook for 2 minutes. Add the garlic and the apricots. Remove from the fire and pour in the stock. Return to gentle heat and whisk until thick. Stir in the ⅓ cup raisins.

Add the vegetables (see preparation page 135) and simmer for 6 or 7 minutes to allow the vegetables to absorb the flavor of the curry. Just before serving, stir in the fresh lime juice.

### Vegetable Preparation

Wash vegetables thoroughly under plentiful cold running water. Scrape the carrots and cut into 1-inch pieces on the bias. Scrape celery with a vegetable peeler to remove the coarse fiber. Cut into pieces to match carrots. Divide cauliflower into small buds. Cut ends off the zucchini and cut into quarter-inch rounds.

Add 1 tablespoon salt to 1 quart water and bring to a boil. Cook vegetables, with the exception of the zucchini, in this order. Carrots—4 to 5 minutes, lift out and drain. In the same water, celery—3 to 4 minutes, lift out and drain. Cauliflower—4 to 5 minutes, lift out and drain. Test each vegetable while cooking because they should be crisp.

Simmer zucchini in the Curry Sauce for 3 to 4 minutes. Add the other vegetables and heat thoroughly. Pile the curried vegetables in the middle of a serving dish with rice at either end. Sprinkle generously with chopped parsley.

*2½ cups chicken stock*
*⅓ cup raisins*
*1 teaspoon lime juice*

**The Vegetables**

*6 medium carrots*
*4 sticks celery*
*1 small cauliflower*
*6 small zucchini*
*1 tablespoon salt*
*3 cups cooked rice*
*1 cup parsley sprigs, chopped*

## COMPOTE OF PEARS WITH SAUCE DIJONNAISE

Peel the pears. Cut a thin slice from the bottom so that the pears will stand upright. Leave the stem intact.

In a large pan with a lid dissolve the sugar in the water. Add the cinnamon sticks, cloves and lemon quarters. Simmer for half an hour with the lid on. Add the pears and simmer gently till soft when pierced with a toothpick. Cooking time will vary with the degree of ripeness of the pears. Do not overcook. Cool in the syrup. Serve in individual glass bowls and spoon a little of the poaching syrup over each. Or serve with Sauce Dijonnaise.

*6 pears, Anjou or Comice, not too ripe*
*3 cups sugar*
*2 quarts water*
*4 sticks cinnamon*
*8 whole cloves*
*1 lemon, cut in quarters*

■ *Note: The poaching syrup may be frozen and used over again.*

## SAUCE DIJONNAISE

Rub the mixed preserves and raspberries through a fine sieve; refrigerate. Serve on top of pears or pass separately.

*½ cup black currant preserves*
*1 10-ounce package frozen raspberries, thawed and drained*

## JACQUES PÉPIN

# A Piquant Chicken Dinner

**MENU**

Vinegar Chicken
Parsley Potatoes
Mother's Apple Tart

Total Cost of Dinner for 6: $5.35

Wine: Beaujolais Côtes-du-Rhône
*(Cost not included)*

*Jacques Pépin has been a professional chef since boyhood. Once chef to Charles de Gaulle, he has worked at many fine French restaurants including the celebrated Le Pavillon in New York. Mr. Pépin is the author of* The Other Half of the Egg *(with Helen McCully), and he writes a monthly column for* House Beautiful.

hicken is probably one of the least expensive meats today and one of the most versatile.

To economize on time, start this menu by preparing the dessert. When the tart is in the oven, you'll have time to prepare the chicken and the potatoes. The entire dinner should then be ready at the same time.

Chicken is best when served as soon as it is ready; the potatoes as well. The chicken and potatoes will taste reheated if cooked in advance (as is often the case in restaurants.) The tart is best served lukewarm.

For a fancier dessert, glaze the top of the tart with apricot jam.

If the menu is served for lunch, a dry white wine would be appropriate.

## VINEGAR CHICKEN

### Poulet Au Vinaigre

Sprinkle the chicken pieces with the salt and pepper. Melt ⅓ stick of butter divided equally between two heavy skillets. When the butter is hot, place the pieces skin side down and brown for a few minutes on medium heat. Turn the pieces and brown the other side. The pieces should be brown all around. It takes about 8 to 10 minutes.

Add the water and ⅓ cup of vinegar, divided equally between both skillets. Cover tightly and cook on medium heat for 20 minutes. Remove the chicken to a serving platter. As soon as the chicken cools somewhat, remove the bone from the breast or pull it off easily, and the piece of the backbone from both legs. It may be considered a little more elegant to remove the bones, but it may certainly be served unboned. Keep the chicken warm on the corner of the stove or in a 180 F. oven. Do not cover or the chicken may taste slightly reheated.

After removing the pieces of chicken from the skillets, add the garlic to one skillet and sauté for one minute. Be careful not to burn the garlic or the sauce will be ruined. Add ⅓ cup of vinegar and boil, making sure that you melt all the solidified juices.

Transfer the liquid to the second skillet and add the

1½ chickens (6 pieces), cut up in parts
¾ teaspoon freshly ground black pepper or 1 teaspoon crushed, green peppercorns
1½ teaspoons salt
⅔ stick unsalted butter
⅓ cup water
⅔ cup red wine vinegar
3 cloves garlic, peeled, crushed, and chopped fine
1 tablespoon tomato paste
1 tablespoon chopped parsley
2 teaspoons freshly chopped tarragon (If tarragon is not available, omit it completely.)

tomato paste to thicken the sauce. Add salt and pepper to taste. The sauce should be peppery. Remove the skillet from the heat and add ⅓ stick butter, bit by bit, with one hand. At the same time, shake the skillet with the other hand so that the butter blends with the sauce. It should yield 1 to 1¼ cups only. Pour it over the chicken, sprinkle with the herbs, and serve immediately.

## PARSLEY POTATOES
### Pommes De Terre Persillées

*3 pounds small potatoes \**
*1 teaspoon salt*
*½ stick unsalted butter*
*4 tablespoons freshly chopped parsley*

*\* If big potatoes are used, cut them into large chunks and trim, producing 30 pieces approximately 1½ inches in diameter.*

Cover the potatoes with cold water. Add the salt and bring to a boil. Boil slowly for about 15 to 18 minutes, or until tender when pierced with a small knife. Drain the potatoes (this is important), place them back in the saucepan over medium heat to evaporate all remaining water. This will give you a very moist and rich-textured potato. Add the butter and parsley and cook just long enough for the butter to melt and coat the potatoes. Serve immediately.

## MOTHER'S APPLE TART
### Tarte Aux Pommes De Ma Mère

**Dough**

*1¼ cups all-purpose flour*
*2 teaspoons baking powder*
*¼ teaspoon salt*
*1 egg*
*3 tablespoons unsalted butter*
*3 tablespoons vegetable shortening*
*2 tablespoons boiling water*

**Filling**

*2–3 Golden or Red Delicious apples—about 1 pound*
*3 tablespoons sugar*
*2 tablespoons unsalted butter*

Preheat oven to 400 F. Place 1 cup of flour, baking powder and salt in a 2-quart mixing bowl; stir lightly. Add egg, butter and shortening and stir to just combine ingredients. Add boiling water and mix only enough for dough to gather into a ball. Sprinkle the remaining ¼ cup flour on a pastry board or marble slab; gently roll the dough into a circle about 12 inches in diameter. (Though the dough is very soft, it can be used right away. If it breaks, patch it with another piece of dough, pressing it into place with your fingers.) Place a 9-inch flan ring on a heavy cookie sheet.

Line with dough, making the top edge a little thicker than the bottom. Trim off excess. (Or, line 9-inch pie pan with dough.)

Peel, core and slice the apples about ¼-inch thick.

Arrange the slices on top of the dough as artfully as you can. Sprinkle with sugar and butter, broken into bits. Place in center of oven and bake from 40 to 60 minutes or until apples are tender and the tart is nicely browned. Before serving, lift off flan ring and with a long spatula, slide tart onto flat platter. (If pie pan is used, place on platter and serve from pan.) Serve luke-warm.

# WILLIAM RICE

# A Vegetarian Menu For Meat Eaters

**MENU**

Hot Salad with Mushrooms and Bean Sprouts
Cauliflower with Curry Sauce
Pakistani Bread Pudding

Total Cost of Dinner for 6: $7.18

Wine: Beer or Tea
(*Cost not included*)

William Rice *is Executive Food Editor of* The Washington Post *and has written food and wine articles for publications in the United States and in England. Mr. Rice served as restaurant critic for* The Washingtonian *magazine and directed a cooking school in Washton, D.C.*

ne of the happiest developments brought on by the desire to economize in the face of high food prices is that one no longer has to be a vegetarian to eat vegetables. While beef prices turned downward toward the end of 1974, the moral and health rationales for decreasing individual meat consumption remain valid. Americans consume too much fat and too many calories and thus endanger their health. American cattle were eating great quantities of grain while people around the world were starving for lack of grain. Vegetables, as a separate course or even a whole meal, should become more popular in this country. I eat meat and plan to continue doing so, but serve less of it when there are several vegetables on the same plate and occasionally enjoy surprising guests by serving them a meal that includes no meat at all.

In the aftermath of the much publicized meat boycott of 1973, consumers did buy less meat. They began to experiment with recipes from foreign cuisines, most notably the Chinese, and to buy more herbs and spices to dress up leftovers.

But so accustomed are we to meated meals that people are uncertain of how to structure a meal that does not include meat as the main course and are even fearful not to serve it. One of the questions I, as a food editor, am invariably asked when I propose a meatless meal as an economy measure is "Will it fill us up?"

The answer is yes. The menu I suggest here, a mushroom and bean sprout salad, followed by cauliflower with a curry sauce and bread pudding, has enough variety and stimulating taste sensations to satisfy all but the most ardent meat eaters. They can satisfy their craving by sneaking off after the meal to a fast food hamburger shop for a quickie. They won't need it though. If in doubt, try serving this for the first time as a weekend luncheon. To round out the meal serve an unusual bread, either the flat Middle Eastern-style rounds sold in groceries or a homemade loaf, perhaps one of the whole meal breads found in James Beard's *Beard on Bread.* Beer or tea are the logical beverages.

The salad is of Chinese derivation, the sauce is English and the dessert comes from Pakistan. Yet all but a couple of the ingredients are sold in supermarkets. For extra economy the mushroom stems can be used in a soup, stuffing or may be sautéed for another meal. Unused curry sauce may be reheated with a few tablespoons of water or wine, then combined with sliced meat or chicken to make a delicious meal of leftovers. It blends particularly well with lamb.

Broccoli could substitute for cauliflower in the main course, reconstituted dried mushrooms can replace fresh in the salad and shredded cabbage might replace the bean sprouts although that would mean a sacrifice in the meal's protein content. If the vegetable for the main course is cooked in water, save the liquid. Like meat broth it makes a nutritious base for soups or sauces.

### HOT SALAD WITH MUSHROOMS AND BEAN SPROUTS

2 tablespoons soy sauce
½ tablespoon sugar
2 tablespoons dry sherry
½ tablespoon dry mustard
¼ teaspoon hot pepper
sauce (optional)
1 tablespoon hoisin sauce
1 tablespoon sesame oil
3 tablespoons peanut or
salad oil
½ pound mushrooms,
cleaned and thinly sliced
4 scallions, white, and green
both, thinly sliced
1½ pounds bean sprouts,
fresh or canned, washed
and drained

Combine soy, sugar, sherry, mustard, pepper and hoisin sauces and sesame oil in a bowl or measuring cup and place on or near the stove.

Heat peanut or salad oil in a large frying pan, high-sided heavy pot or wok. Add mushrooms and scallion and sauté over high heat until juices begin to come from the mushrooms. Add bean sprouts and toss until they are heated through, 45 seconds to a minute. Pour liquid ingredients from bowl over vegetables and toss for an additional 30 seconds. Turn into a bowl or platter and serve at once.

### CAULIFLOWER WITH CURRY SAUCE

3 pounds cauliflower, leaves
trimmed and broken or cut
into sections or flowerets
2 bay leaves
Salt

**For the Sauce:**

¼ cup butter
1 small onion, finely
chopped
½ apple, peeled and finely
chopped
4 teaspoons curry powder,
or to taste
3½ tablespoons all-purpose
flour

Make the sauce first. Melt butter in a pan, add onion and apple and cook gently for 5 to 6 minutes. Stir in curry powder and flour, cook for a minute, then add heated stock. Bring to a simmer, stirring, until a sauce is formed. Add remaining ingredients, cover and cook over low heat for 20 to 30 minutes. (This may be done ahead.)

While sauce heats, place cauliflower in boiling salted water with bay leaves (or steam it over the water) and cook until just tender to a knife-point. Arrange cooked cauliflower on a platter, spoon sauce over and serve.

2½ cups chicken stock or
bouillon (or vegetable
broth)
2 tablespoons chutney,
chopped
2 tablespoons brown sugar
Juice of ½ lemon
½ teaspoon salt
¼ cup raisins

## PAKISTANI BREAD PUDDING

If bread is somewhat stale, it will help, not harm the
dish. Heat oil in a large frying pan. Fry bread slices
without crowding pan until browned on both sides.
Drain on paper toweling.

Lightly oil a small baking dish and fit bread slices
into it. Heat half-and-half with condensed milk, salt and
saffron to the point of a boil, then simmer for 5 minutes
or until liquid thickens. Pour over toasted bread, place
silver paper on top and scatter nuts over all. Bake in a
350 F. oven for 45 minutes. Serve warm or prepare
ahead and serve at room temperature.

1 loaf bread (the type used
for submarine sandwiches is
best), cut into ½-inch-wide
slices
¼ cup vegetable oil for
frying
1 pint half-and-half cream
½ 13-ounce can condensed
milk
Pinch salt
¼ teaspoon saffron stems,
pounded to a powder
2 or 3 sheets silver paper, *
optional
¼ cup slivered almonds
¼ cup pistachios, peeled
and chopped

* Silver paper is sold in
Indian and Pakistani spe-
cialty food stores for about
$1.25 for 3 sheets.

## PAUL RUBINSTEIN

# Leftovers With A Slavic Flavor

**MENU**

Hot Beet Borscht with Sour Cream
Polish Hunter's Stew (Bigos)
Buttered Steamed Potatoes
Fresh Cranberry Kissel

Total Cost of Dinner for 6: $9.64

Wine: German Reisling or Beer
*(Cost not included)*

Paul Rubinstein, *son of the world famous pianist, Artur Rubinstein, is a stockbroker and a devoted cook. He is the author of two cookbooks,* Feasts for Two *and* The Night Before Cookbook. *Described by Craig Claiborne as "a cooking genius," Mr. Rubinstein is a member of the faculty of The Good Cooking School.*

his economy menu is versatile primarily because of the Polish Hunter's Stew (Bigos). Its ingredients may be altered with no damage to the end result. First and foremost among allowable substitutions is the use of leftover meat. Any cooked meat will work fine, except for poultry. Just cube and add. Bacon is an essential ingredient because of its smoky taste, and some sort of sausage. If you cannot find the prescribed sausages, then cut some salami into cubes and substitute. If you like, use cooked spare ribs or short ribs of beef as long as you don't mind the bones.

The proportions of sauerkraut to meat may be altered to make the stew either richer or lighter. Other permissible substitutions are cider, white wine or beer for the apple juice; sliced leeks for the onion; pimientos or green peppers for a third of the stewed tomatoes. If you don't like potatoes as an accompaniment, serve rice or egg noodles instead.

For entertaining, Bigos is a dream of ease. I have personally fed 75 people with this dish prepared in two huge pots two days in advance and reheated for a late supper.

A few words about the beet borscht: I prefer using fresh beets, and rarely have any trouble finding them. However, a perfectly good taste may be achieved by using canned beets. If you use canned beets, look for the largest size beets, avoiding cans labeled with words like "tiny" or "baby," and employ *every drop* of the liquid for the soup.

You may find that the kissel is too sweet or too tart, depending on your own taste. Feel free to add or subtract sugar after once having tried it as described here.

No matter what changes you make or what leftovers you use, there is no way that the menu can be made to cost very much to serve!

## HOT BEET BORSCHT WITH SOUR CREAM

Cut off the tops and wash the beets well under cold running water.

Set up a steaming platform in a large stock pot over about 3 quarts of water. Place the washed beets on the platform, cover, bring the water to a boil and steam until the beets are tender (1 to 1½ hours).

*8 medium-sized beets (2 to 3 inches diameter)*
*4 European dried mushrooms or 1 tablespoon powdered mushrooms*
*3 cups beef broth or beef*

consommé (*canned or
homemade*)
*2 tablespoons white vinegar*
*1 cup shredded cabbage*
*½ cup minced onion*
*½ teaspoon salt*
*¼ teaspoon freshly ground
black pepper*
*½ pint sour cream*
*3 hard cooked eggs
(optional)*

While beets are steaming, cover the dried mushrooms with one cup of boiling water and let them soak.

When beets are done remove them from the steaming platform, let them cool a few minutes, then peel them. The skin should come off quite easily. Reserve the cooking liquid.

Strain the cooking liquid twice through cheesecloth, then put it in a large saucepan. If there is more than about 6 cups of this liquid, boil it down to that amount.

Grate the peeled beets through the coarsest blade of your grater and add them to the saucepan.

Add the liquid from the mushrooms to the saucepan. Chop the soaked mushrooms very fine and add them too. (If you are using the powdered mushrooms, mix the powder with a little of the broth until a paste is formed, add the paste to the saucepan.)

Add the beef broth, vinegar, cabbage, onion, salt and pepper to the saucepan, bring to a simmer and cook uncovered for about 30 minutes.

Serve in soup plates with a generous spoonful of sour cream in each plate.

Optional garnish: peel the hard cooked eggs and cut them in half. Float one half egg in each plate of borscht.

## POLISH HUNTER'S STEW
## BIGOS

This dish is ideal for entertaining for several reasons. In addition to being inexpensive, it can be prepared well in advance and reheated when needed. In fact, it benefits from standing overnight and reheating. Leftovers may be frozen in a plastic container for later use. Because of its contents no vegetables or salad is needed as an accompaniment—except for a starch (potatoes)—and it is quite lean and very nourishing, therefore excellent for diets.

In a large stock pot or casserole assemble the sauerkraut with its liquid, the apple chunks, stewed tomatoes with their liquid, the sliced onion, chopped cabbage, tomato paste, bacon pieces, bay leaf, garlic, thyme, brown sugar, pepper and apple juice.

Heat over a high flame until simmering, then reduce heat and cook at a gentle simmer, partially covered, for about 2 hours, stirring occasionally.

*3 pounds sauerkraut*
*3 apples, cored and cut in
chunks, but not peeled*
*1 20-ounce can stewed
tomatoes*
*1 large onion, peeled and
sliced*
*¼ of a head of cabbage,
chopped*
*2 tablespoons tomato paste*
*6 slices of bacon, cut into
1-inch lengths*
*1 bay leaf*
*1 clove garlic, peeled and
crushed*
*1 tablespoon ground thyme*
*½ cup brown sugar*
*1 teaspoon freshly ground
black pepper*
*1 cup apple juice*
*1 cup Polish, Hungarian or
Spanish garlic sausage,*

Add the sausage and meat, stirring well to distribute the meat throughout, and continue cooking at the same pace for 1 hour more.

Serve hot, or if prepared in advance, reheat over low flame allowing at least 30 minutes.

*sliced into ¼-inch slices*
*3 cups cubed leftover cooked meat such as beef, pork or ham or any mixture of the three ***

** See note following recipe for meat portions.*

■ *Note: Meat portions for Polish Hunter's Stew (Bigos):*

### Beef

Have butcher cut beef into ½-inch cubes. Brown the beef cubes in their own juices in a heavy iron skillet on all sides. Add to the Bigos at the appropriate point in the recipe.

*1½ pounds cubed stewing beef (makes 3 cups)*

### Ham

Cut the cooked ham into ½-inch cubes. Add to the Bigos at the appropriate point in the recipe. You may use partially cooked cured or smoked ham instead of fully cooked ham. Both the ham and the smoked pork will cook long enough in the Bigos after being added in any case. Add to the Bigos at the appropriate point in the recipe.

*1½ pounds cooked ham— whole piece, not slices (makes 3 cups)*

### Smoked Pork Loin

Cut the pork loin into ½-inch cubes. Add to the *bigos* at the appropriate point in the recipe.

*1½-pound piece of smoked pork loin (makes 3 cups)*

### BUTTERED STEAMED POTATOES

Peel and wash the potatoes in cold water.

Place the potatoes on a steaming platform over at least 2 inches of water in a stock pot. Bring the water to a boil, cover, and steam about 30 to 40 minutes until potatoes are tender but not falling apart.

When done, remove the potatoes to a warm serving dish. Melt the butter and add the salt to it.

Pour the warm melted butter over the potatoes, sprinkle with the chopped parsley, and keep warm until serving time.

*3 pounds boiling potatoes*
*6 tablespoons butter*
*½ teaspoon salt*
*1 tablespoon freshly chopped parsley*

### FRESH CRANBERRY KISSEL

Wash the berries well and remove any bits of stems. Combine the berries and water in a saucepan, bring to a boil, reduce heat and simmer gently for 15 minutes.

Transfer the contents of the saucepan to a blender (in at least two shifts), blend to a purée, and return to

*4 cups fresh cranberries*
*4 cups water*
*3 tablespoons cornstarch*
*1½ cups granulated sugar*
*1 teaspoon ground cinnamon*

*½ pint heavy cream,
chilled (optional)
2 tablespoons granulated
sugar (optional)*

pan. Alternative: rub the cranberry mixture through a fine sieve.

Dip out about ½-cup of the liquid, blend with the cornstarch until completely dissolved, and return to pan.

Add the sugar and the cinnamon, bring to a simmer and mix well until sugar is completely melted.

Remove from heat and pour into decorative serving bowl or individual bowls. Allow to cool to room temperature, then chill in refrigerator until serving time.

Optional: shortly before serving, beat the heavy cream with the 2 tablespoons sugar until it forms stiff peaks. Serve with the kissel.

■ *Note: This dessert does not require gelatin. The binding agent is the cornstarch which results in a soft, thick consistency aided by chilling, but not a rubbery gelatinous one. It may be served with whipped cream or with plain sweet cream.*

## HARVEY STEIMAN

# A Rich, Refreshing Chicken Dinner

**MENU**

Bacon-Sour Cream Quiche
Fall Salad
Casserole-Roasted Chicken with Zucchini
Grapefruit Sherbet

Total Cost of Dinner for 6: $12.50

Bonus Recipes: Omelet Fillings

Wine: California Zinfandel
*(Cost not included)*

Harvey Steiman *is Food Editor of* The Miami Herald. *His weekly column, "The Budget Gourmet," presents menus centered around those food items attractively priced in the market each week. He has taught cooking classes and lectured on wine and restaurants at Florida International University's food and hotel school.*

here would the budget-minded cook be without the chicken? Whichever came first, both the chicken and its eggs are versatile mainstays that do not make much of a dent in the billfold.

In my column, "The Budget Gourmet," I scan the supermarket advertisements each week for lower priced items, then try to build a dinner or luncheon menu around them. There are times when nothing looks cheap, and that is when we turn to omelets, crêpes, quiches, or any of the hundreds of things that can be done with eggs or their parents.

As much as I love a good roast chicken, I have come to prefer a different way of cooking a whole chicken in the oven: casserole-roasting. The chicken steams in butter and its own juices, plus those of whatever vegetables cook in the casserole with it. The results are tender and flavorful, yet the process involves a minimum of fuss.

The recipe here uses zucchini because it is generally available year round. However, most vegetables can be substituted. Those that cook quickly, like peas, must be added halfway through cooking time. Mushrooms are particularly good. Vegetables that cook quickly can also be sliced thicker. Whatever you do, the vegetables take on a marvelous flavor from the chicken juices.

The quiche was a happy discovery when we found pint cartons of sour cream on sale. We substituted sour cream for heavy cream in a basic quiche recipe and discovered a flavor entirely different from any quiche I had tasted before. It has a creamy smooth texture and a sort of "bite" unlike anything you might expect from cheese. With a salad, a loaf of bread and a bottle of wine, it makes a fine dinner on its own.

The fall salad has become sort of our "house" salad ever since a leftover apple found its way into a plain green salad one day. For my money, bibb is the finest type of lettuce produced in the United States. It is not a rigid requirement for this salad, however—any leaf lettuce from romaine to Boston is excellent.

Grapefruit juice freshly squeezed from the fruit of a nearby tree is one of the great rewards for living in Florida. There ought to be some way, I reasoned, to make a good sherbet from it, but the results, using standard sherbet recipes, were always disappointing.

Most sherbet recipes call for additional water or milk but grapefruit is less intensely flavored so as little liquid as possible results in a tangy and somewhat delicate sherbet.

In shopping for this meal, keep these few things in mind:

The chickens should be between three and four pounds. Larger chickens have more meat in proportion to bones and they are generally a little older and consequently more flavorful. Above four pounds, the skin starts getting tough and the bird becomes more suited to poaching than to roasting. Look to see that the breastbone is not sticking out. Broad-breasted, loose-skinned birds are best. If the chicken is in a bag, watch out for loose juices. This means the chicken has probably been frozen and thawed. Yellow-skinned chickens used to mean they were corn-fed, but this no longer holds. Nowadays, powdered marigold added to the chickens' feed does the same thing.

Grapefruit season runs from November through May and peaks in February. Seedless grapefruit tends to have less flavor than seeded varieties. To make juice, both types must be strained, anyway, after squeezing. When shopping, remember that heavier fruit for its size is juicier. Color means nothing since most of the fruit that is destined to be shipped is sprayed with artificial coloring. Weight is most important. Look for larger, heavier fruit.

### BACON-SOUR CREAM QUICHE

**The Pastry**

*1 cup sifted all-purpose flour*
*½ teaspoon salt*
*½ teaspoon sugar*
*⅓ cup butter*
*2–2½ tablespoons ice water*

#### The Pastry

Preheat oven to 400 F.

Mix flour, salt and sugar. Cut butter into flour until mixture forms something resembling meal. Gradually sprinkle with ice water, adding only enough to hold dough together in a ball.

Refrigerate for one hour. Then roll out between two pieces of wax paper edge to edge. Refrigerate a few minutes longer before peeling off wax paper and gently pressing dough into 9 or 10-inch tart pan.

**The Filling**

*9- or 10-inch pie or tart shell*
*¼ pound bacon*
*2 cups sour cream*
*4 eggs*

#### The Filling

Preheat oven to 400 F.

Cut bacon into ½-inch pieces. Fry over moderate heat until crisp. Drain on paper towels and allow to cool.

Prick tart shell in several places with a fork. Bake it 10 minutes. Remove from oven.

Allow sour cream to come to room temperature. Place in mixing bowl. Beat eggs and add them to sour cream, stirring to combine thoroughly. Add reserved bacon and pepper. Pour into tart shell, taking care to distribute bacon evenly. Carefully float slices of zucchini in an attractive pattern on surface of quiche.

Place quiche in oven. After 15 minutes, reduce heat to 375 F. Bake 10 to 20 minutes longer, or until top surface feels firm when pressed lightly.

*Freshly ground black pepper*
*½ pound zucchini, sliced thin (optional)*

■ *Variations: Instead of zucchini, peel, core and slice a tart green apple thinly. Arrange slices around edge of quiche and sprinkle with grated Romano cheese.*

*For a more delicately flavored quiche, replace 1 cup sour cream with 1 cup milk.*

*For a more delicately textured quiche, replace all of the sour cream with plain yogurt.*

## FALL SALAD

Spread diced apples around bottom of salad bowl. Sprinkle with juice of lemon. Scatter minced scallion on top of apple. Break lettuce into bite-sized pieces and dry thoroughly. Place on top of apples and scallions, sprinkle with tarragon and refrigerate until ready to serve (but no more than 2 hours).

Sprinkle with enough olive oil to coat all the lettuce leaves lightly, about ¼ cup. Toss from bottom up. Add salt and pepper, freshly ground, to taste.

*2 small, tart apples, diced*
*Juice of 1 lemon*
*1 scallion, trimmed and minced*
*2 quarts bibb or leaf lettuce*
*1 teaspoon dried tarragon or 1 tablespoon fresh tarragon*
*¼ cup olive oil*
*Salt*
*Pepper*

■ *Note: Apples will keep, sprinkled with lemon juice, for several hours but lettuce will lose crispness if kept too long.*

*If you are a bit of a showman, make the salad at the table, chopping the apples just before preparing the salad in this order: break lettuce into bowl, coat with oil and toss; add tarragon, scallions, lemon juice and apples; toss again; add salt and pepper, toss and serve.*

## CASSEROLE-ROASTED CHICKEN WITH ZUCCHINI

Rinse and dry chickens thoroughly. Peel garlic cloves and slice in half lengthwise. Place two cloves in cavity of each chicken with ½ teaspoon tarragon or 2 tea-

*2 3–3½-pound roasting chickens*
*4 garlic cloves*

*1 teaspoon dried tarragon
or 4 teaspoons parsley
9 tablespoons butter
3 tablespoons vegetable oil
2 medium onions, sliced
¼ cup brandy
3 cups zucchini, cut in
¼-inch slices
3 cups carrots, cut in
⅛-inch slices
Salt
Pepper*

spoons parsley. Tie or truss chickens firmly. Preheat oven to 350 F.

In a heavy casserole large enough to accommodate both chickens, heat 3 tablespoons butter and 3 tablespoons oil. (If you do not have a large enough casserole, use two casseroles and divide butter and oil accordingly.) Over moderate heat, when butter foam subsides, brown chicken lightly on all sides, turning with two wooden spoons. Take care not to tear skin. This process should take 10 to 12 minutes.

Remove chickens from casserole and pour off what will now be burned butter. Turn to lower heat and melt remaining butter. Cook onions until limp but not browned. Replace chickens, breast up. Flame chickens with brandy, then distribute vegetables around chicken. Sprinkle with salt and pepper, cover tightly and place in oven.

Cook 1 hour and 10 minutes to 1½ hours. Cooking time depends on size of chickens. Test for doneness by trying to jiggle leg joint—it should move easily—or by piercing thigh joint. The juices should run clear yellow with no pink or red. Remove cover and allow chickens to brown during last 10 minutes of cooking.

Remove chickens to serving platter, untie them and remove garlic cloves. Carve chickens and serve with vegetables on the side. If chicken seems a little dry, spoon some of the pan drippings over it.

This casserole-roasted chicken is very good simply warmed up the next day. But save some of the pan juices to use as gravy.

■ *Variations: To serve six, a capon of 6 to 8 pounds may be substituted for the two fryers in this menu. Capons are castrated male birds, bred to be tender and meaty. Unfortunately, most markets get them only frozen and they cost more per pound than fryers or roasters. Given a dinner for six persons, then, if you are going to use fryers or roasters, two are necessary.*

*Another variation would be to replace zucchini with sliced fresh mushrooms, stuffing the chicken with as many mushroom slices as possible and scattering the rest around the casserole.*

*Or, omit zucchini altogether and when chicken is cooked, strain pan juices into a medium skillet, add 1 small can drained minced clams, and cook over high heat for 1 minute; add ¼ cup heavy cream mixed with 1 tablespoon arrowroot or cornstarch and stir until thickened. Serve with chicken as sauce.*

*You may also substitute any sliceable vegetable for the zucchini. Slice quicker-cooking vegetables thicker.*

### GRAPEFRUIT SHERBET

Clear a space on flat surface in freezer large enough to accommodate a pan or metal mixing bowl 1 quart or larger.

2 cups freshly squeezed grapefruit juice, strained
Juice of 1 lemon, strained
¼ cup Cointreau or other orange liqueur
1 cup light corn syrup
2 egg whites

Combine grapefruit juice, lemon juice, liqueur and corn syrup in pan. Beat until thoroughly blended. Place in freezer until it freezes around the top and edges, about three hours.

Beat egg whites until they hold soft peaks. Do not overbeat. Remove pan from freezer. Working quickly, beat sherbet with a large wire whisk or electric mixer until smooth, then beat in egg whites. Return to freezer until firm, about another two hours.

Remove from freezer again and mix with a spoon to combine egg whites—which have probably floated to the top—with rest of sherbet. Return to freezer until ready to serve.

Unless your freezer is very cold, the sherbet should scoop well without having to soften it first. Scoop or spoon into sherbet glasses and serve immediately.

■ *Note: The liqueur is important to keep the sherbet from freezing solid too easily. The egg whites help in this regard and they also improve the texture.*

*This is one sherbet that tastes better the second day. Once completely frozen, it can be packed, covered, in a deep one-quart container. It is also delicious sprinkled with a little rum.*

*For a festive touch, poke a sprig of mint into each serving, or garnish with a grapefruit segment, mandarin orange segment or candied orange peel.*

■ *Bonus Recipes*

### THREE OMELET FILLINGS

The leftover meat from the second chicken in Chicken with Zucchini (recipe page 159) can be pulled from the bones, diced, and will easily serve four the next day as an omelet filling. Here are three fillings designed to use up this leftover chicken:

### Chicken and Bacon Filling

Render three or four slices of chopped bacon in a small saucepan. Add a tablespoon of flour and cook, stirring, 4 to 5 minutes over moderate heat. Add ¾ cup milk and cook, stirring, until thickened. Add chicken, stir and simmer 10 minutes. Just before making omelets, stir in one tablespoon heavy cream.

### Chicken and Sour Cream Filling

Sauté chicken lightly in a little butter. Add ½ cup or more sour cream and just warm it up. Season with salt and pepper.

### Chicken and Onion Filling

Combine diced chicken with 2 tablespoons minced onion simmered in ¼ cup heavy cream until reduced by one-half, or ½ cup chicken stock reduced by three-quarters. Season with salt, pepper and a pinch of nutmeg.

# NICOLA ZANGHI

# A Lusty Italian Supper

**MENU**

Mozzarella in Carozza
Italian Beef Stew
Fettucine
Romaine Salad
Spumoni Messina

Total Cost of Dinner for 6: $17.20

Wine: California Zinfandel *or* California Pinot Noir
*(Cost not included)*

Bonus Recipe: Egg Drop Soup

Nicola Zanghi, *a graduate of Pratt Institute and New York Community College in Culinary Arts, works with his father at their own restaurant, Restaurant Zanghi, on Long Island, N.Y. Mr. Zanghi is well-versed in all types of cooking, but his specialty is the fine Italian cooking of the Northern Piedmont area. He has taught cooking at New York University and at New York City Community College, and demonstrated various types of cooking on a daily morning television show.*

professional chef has always had to work within a prescribed food cost. He must utilize every morsel of food with as little waste as possible. The very economic success of the restaurant depends upon the savings created by the chef.

This menu is most satisfying—especially the beef on a brisk day. The dishes progress from a light, almost airy appetizer, to a hearty stew with noodles, a lemony salad, and a most refreshing dessert. These specialties are a subtle blend of aromatic seasonings, differences in texture that create an overall eye appeal. It is what a meal should be.

The appetizer wakes up the palate with crisp, fried bread. Watch how the mozzarella just oozes and runs when cut. But one will not find himself too full for the next course.

Our classic Northern Italian beef stew will win over any guest. Versions of it will be found all over Northern Italy in small lodges at the start of the hunting season. After a day in the woods, the *cacciatore* is satiated with *stufatino*. The herbs, the aromatics, the wine permeate the entire household while simmering.

Salad is always eaten after the main course in Europe. This tradition came about so that the dressings would not conflict with wines. Try eating the greens at this point and you will notice that the lemony taste will cleanse the palate.

Sicily is renowned for its *gelati* and *sorbeti*. They are the finest ice creams produced, with a texture and somewhat chewy quality that is unique. *Spuma* in Italian means foam and in the Spumoni Messina you will notice a fine, porous grain in each slice. The grain is colorful when studded with the candied fruits and the rich shading of the eggs and cream.

## MOZZARELLA IN CAROZZA

*Carozza* means coach: We'll cut the bread in rounds for the coach's wheels.

Heat oils in heavy saucepan. Beat eggs, salt and freshly ground pepper. Place 6 slices of cheese on top of 6 slices of bread; cover with remaining 6 slices of bread. Using a 3-inch cookie or hors d'oeuvre cutter, press

*2 cups vegetable oil*
*½ cup olive oil*
*2 eggs*
*Salt*
*Freshly ground pepper*
*6 slices (½-pound) mozzarella or Swiss or Muenster*

*12 slices 2-day-old
white bread
Flour
2 lemons cut in wedges
Parsley sprigs*

down and cut rounds. (If you don't have a cutter, you can fashion it from a small can.)

Flour these rounds, dip in eggs, then into the oils. Make sure oils are slightly smoking. Using tongs, spatula or spoon, turn them over and fry until golden brown. Remove from oil, drain on towels, place on heated dish. Garnish with lemon wedges and parsley sprigs.

■ *Note: Retain the egg batter and bread trimmings to use in our Bonus Recipe on page 168.*

*The oils may be strained and reused for future frying.*

## ITALIAN BEEF STEW

### Stufatino di Manzo

*½ cup vegeteable oil
5½ pounds "semi-boneless"
chuck roast cut into
1½-inch cubes
½ cup olive oil
2 cups diced onion
½ cup flour
2 cups dry, red wine
4 cups celery, cut into
1-inch pieces
4 cups carrots, split lengthwise and cut into 1-inch
pieces
4 cups plum tomatoes,
peeled and cut into
1-inch pieces
1 cup tomato purée
Water
¼ teaspoon thyme
¼ teaspoon freshly ground
nutmeg
Freshly ground pepper
2 tablespoons salt*

**Herb Bouquet \***

*4 cloves
4 bay leaves
2 garlic cloves, crushed*

*\* To make the bouquet, place the ingredients in a small 4 x 4-inch square of cheese cloth tied with string to be secured to side of stewing pot when indicated in recipe.*

Bone meat, clean nerves and gristle and cut into cubes. This should yield 3½ pounds meat.

Heat vegetable oil in 18-inch skillet. When oil is hot (slight smoke), add meat. Stir and toss a few times over high heat until evenly browned. Remove, place in colander and wash with warm water. This will clean all suet and impurities.

Heat olive oil in a 1½-gallon heavy stewing pot. Over high heat sauté diced onion until limp and translucent. Add beef, sprinkle flour, and mix with wooden spoon for a few minutes allowing flour to cook. Add red wine. When mixture is thick and purple, wine will be cooked. Add celery, carrots, tomatoes, purée and water. Reduce heat to simmer. Add thyme, nutmeg, herb bouquet, and 12 turns of the pepper mill. Let cook 1¼ hours. Season with approximately two tablespoons of salt. Allow 15 minutes additional for salt to cook in.

This dish may be prepared in advance and kept refrigerated. It may also be braised in a 325 F. oven for 1½ hours.

■ *Note: Save carrot, celery peelings and leftover beef bones and trimmings for Bonus Recipe on page 168.*

*The beef broth from the stew can also be reduced and turned into an extract for sauces.*

## FETTUCINE

Boil fettucine in salted water 7 minutes. (It is important that the fettucine be stirred with a fork several times while boiling to prevent the noodles from sticking.) Drain, add butter and oil and mix until melted. Keep in warm area until ready to serve.

Place noodles on same plate as stew and serve some of the rich sauce made from the meat dish on top of the pasta.

*1-pound package egg noodles*
*4 tablespoons butter*
*2 tablespoons vegetable oil*
*1 tablespoon salt*

## ROMAINE SALAD
### Insalada di Romana

Allow garlic to sit overnight in oil. Cut or tear lettuce into 1-inch strips and place in bowl. Mix oil and juice, pour over salad and add salt and pepper.

■ *Note: Retain the outer leaves for Bonus Recipe on page 168.*

*Or the outer leaves or trimmings may also be frozen and, when a sufficient quantity has accumulated, they can be steamed for serving as a most economical vegetable. Just season with butter, cheese or garlic.*

*2 garlic cloves, crushed*
*⅔ cup olive oil*
*2 heads romaine lettuce (well washed)*
*⅓ cup fresh lemon juice*
*Salt*
*Freshly ground pepper*

## SPUMONI MESSINA *

In heavy saucepan cook sugar and water till 230 F. (soft ball stage) or till almost clear. While this is cooking, beat eggs in stainless steel or porcelain bowl.

When sugar is ready, pour it into the eggs in a steady stream, a little at a time, while whisking. Constantly beat until this mixture has cooled to room temperature. Fold in whipped cream and remaining ingredients. Will fill a 6-cup mold. Must be frozen at least eight hours.

Unmold under warm, not hot, water.

■ *Note: Remember that with the extracts as well as the liqueurs, the object is to lace or enhance the spumoni's flavor, not to overpower.*

*Spumoni may be made several days in advance and kept frozen.*

*½ cup sugar*
*2 tablespoons water*
*4–5 eggs*
*½ pint whipping cream, beaten stiff*
*Grated rind ½ orange*
*Grated rind ½ lemon*

### Flavorings

*4 tablespoons candied fruit*
*1 tablespoon pure vanilla extract*
*1 teaspoon Strega*
*1 teaspoon Galliano*
*1 teaspoon dark rum*

* *If there is any difficulty in obtaining the mentioned liqueurs for the spumoni, certain extracts can be substituted with great success. I recommend the use of almond, anise, cinnamon, lemon, orange, rum or mocha. Perhaps just ½ teaspoon of any four of the above.*

■ *Bonus Recipe*

**EGG DROP SOUP**
**Straciatella**

From the previous recipes retain the following ingredients:

**From Mozzarella in Carozza**

Strain the egg batter and retain ½ cup.

Dice the bread trimmings into ½-inch cubes and fry in previously used oil until lightly brown. Drain on towels, retain.

**From Beef Stew**

Save carrot and celery peelings and the two pounds of beef bones and trimmings.

The beef bones and trimmings should be blanched to remove impurities, suet and blood. To "blanch," cover the bones with cold water and bring to a boil. Drain and wash. They will stay refrigerated for several days.

**From Romaine Salad**

When cleaning the greens, remove the outer leaves and trim away any discolored parts. Wash well. Boil, covered, with ¼ teaspoon salt for 10 minutes. Drain and cool. Can be refrigerated for several days.

**For the Soup**

*2½ pounds blanched beef bones and trimmings*
*2½ quarts cold water*
*Carrot and celery shavings*
*2 garlic cloves, crushed*
*2 bay leaves*
*3 cloves*
*8 peppercorns*
*Leftover egg batter*
*1 teaspoon salt*
*Steamed salad greens cut into ½-inch pieces*
*Croutons made from bread trimmings*

Combine all ingredients except egg batter, salt, greens and croutons.

Let simmer in saucepan for 2 hours, skimming impurities from top from time to time. Should reduce to approximately 1½ quarts when drained.

Bring broth to a boil. Add salad greens. Allow to simmer 10 minutes. Bring mixture to full rolling boil and drop the egg mixture into it through fine strainer. Let boil for 3 minutes while vigorously stirring to prevent coagulation of the eggs and to have small egg drops.

Season with approximately 1 teaspoon salt. Garnish with croutons. Will yield 6 cups.

# COOKBOOK INDEX